THE AFFINITY RESEARCH GROUP MODEL

Creating and Maintaining Effective Research Teams

Ann Q. Gates
Steve Roach
Elsa Y. Villa
Kerrie Kephart
Connie Della-Piana
Gabriel Della-Piana

The University of Texas at El Paso

IEEE Computer Society Order Number B3424
ISBN 0-7695-3424-4 / 978-0-7695-3424-4

Additional copies may be ordered from:

IEEE Computer Society
Customer Service Center
10662 Los Vaqueros Circle
PO Box 3014
Los Alamitos, CA 90720-1314
USA
Tel: + 1 800 272 6657
Fax: + 1 714 821 4641
http://www.computer.org

IEEE Computer Society
Asia/Pacific Office
KFK Bldg.
2-14-14 Minami-Aoyama
Minato-ku, Tokyo 107-0062
JAPAN
Tel: + 81 3 3408 3118
Fax: + 81 3 3408 3553
tokyo.ofc@computer.org

The production of this book and
associated workshops were supported by
a SEED grant from the
IEEE New Initiatives Committee

Original research performed
under a grant from the
National Science Foundation

TABLE OF CONTENTS

Preface i
- Foundational Ideas
- An Integrated Research Environment
- Universal Benefits
- Using This Guide
- A Content Overview
- Acknowledgments

Chapter 1: What Is an Affinity Research Group? 1
- Affinity Research Group Components
- Five Elements of Cooperation
  - Positive Interdependence
  - Face-to-face Promotive Interaction
  - Individual and Group Accountability
  - Professional Skills
  - Group Processing

Chapter 2: Theory Behind the Model 9
- Cooperative Learning
- Situated Learning

Chapter 3: First Steps 13
- Define a Core Purpose
- Promote Student Connections
- Apply Effective Management Practices
- Joining the Group

Chapter 4: The Orientation 17
- Preparation
- Foundational Elements
  - Student and Faculty Introductions
  - Philosophy and Goals
  - Cooperative Team Skills
  - Research Activities and Skills
  - Competing Concerns

Chapter 5: Project Management 25
- Group Focus
- Resource Management
- Networking
  - Internal
  - External
- Day-to-day Operations
  - Research Project Definition
  - Defined Deliverables
  - Group Meetings
  - Process Improvement
  - Risk Management

Chapter 6: Structured Skills Development 35
- Create a Research Poster
- Write a Technical Report
- Discuss Technical Papers
- Critique Work of Others
- Formulate Technical Questions
- Define Timelines
- Give a Technical Presentation

Develop Expertise
Support Existing Research Projects
Learn from Others
Work in Pairs
Present a Chalk Talk
Chapter 7: Evaluating the Research Experience 47
Purposes of Evaluation
Use of Findings
Formative Evaluation: How Can We Improve?
Summative Evaluation: Have We Succeeded?
An Evaluation Framework
Formulation: Laying the Groundwork
Most Important Driver: Evaluation Questions
Choosing Methods or Approaches to Collect Information
Backward Tracing
Real-Time Monitoring
Implementation Characterization
Peer Review
Applying Plan-Do-Check-Act
References 59
Appendices 63
Appendix A: Group Management 63
Project Summary
Task Assignment Form
Project Status Report
Research Assistant Agreement
Appendix B: Group Meetings 71
Meeting Record
Example Meeting Roles and Procedures
Observation Forms
Appendix C: Templates 75
Thesis Proposal
Journal Paper Summary
Literature Review Guidelines
Literature Review Summary
Tips for Writing a Research Abstract
Proposal Critique
Paper Critique
Presentation Critique Form 1 and Form 2
Conference/Trip Report
Appendix D: Orientation Support Materials 87
Sample Agenda for a Four-Hour Orientation
Task/Maintenance Questionnaire
Nominal Group Technique
Desired Attributes of an Engineer: Boeing Commercial Airplane Group
An Affective Code of Cooperation
Appendix E: Outreach Materials 99
Outreach Activity Documentation Template
Example Documentation: Be a Robot

PREFACE

Since the 1990s, undergraduate research has been helping students identify the skills and knowledge they will need to successfully participate in research projects and appreciate the rewards of graduate study. Indeed, a 2004 study (Seymour et al., 2004), funded by the National Science Foundation (NSF) to analyze the benefits of undergraduate research, found that it increased students' confidence in three areas:

- their ability to do research,
- their professional self-image ("feeling like a scientist"), and
- their skill in presenting and defending research.

It also provided a venue for

- establishing a mentoring relationship with faculty and
- enhancing peer and professional collegiality.

Of the many approaches used to develop and administer university research programs (www.cur.org), two represent unique models to stimulate and enhance the undergraduate research experience by creating learning or practice communities. The Research Communications Studio at the University of South Carolina uses an active learning environment and recognizes that cognition is distributed among members of a research group (Donath et al., 2005). The Affinity Research Group (ARG)—the model represented in this handbook—uses a cooperative learning approach to involve students with diverse backgrounds (Kephart et al., 2008; Gates et al., 1997a).

The heart of the Affinity Research Group Model is the deliberate development of skills that, when applied, results in a highly effective team.

An ARG is a team of faculty mentors, undergraduates, and graduates who work together as peers to solve research problems and who promote the development and success of each team member.

Benefits of Undergraduate Research

Students involved in research

- become lifelong learners,
- attain a higher level of competence in their area of study,
- develop technical and communication skills,
- understand methods and process of research,
- make informed judgments about technical matters, and
- communicate and work in teams.

Foundational Ideas

In 1995, University of Texas at El Paso (UTEP) faculty Andrew Bernat, Ann Quiroz Gates, and Sergio Cabrera developed the ARG model with the goal of retaining and advancing students from computer science and electrical and computer engineering into graduate school.

The ARG model integrates two foundational ideas. The first is that interaction among students and faculty outside the classroom increases the likelihood that stu-

Valuable Skills

Research involvement contributes to skills desired by employers, including

- learning to learn,
- listening and oral communication,
- reading, writing, and computation,
- adaptability (creative thinking and problem solving),
- personal management (self-esteem, goal setting, personal and career development),
- group effectiveness (interpersonal skills, negotiation, and team work), and
- organizational effectiveness and leadership.

dents will persist to graduation (Astin, 1985; Rodriguez, 1994; Tinto et al., 1993). The second is that cooperative learning techniques maximize student learning and efficacy (Johnson and Johnson, 1989).

Because UTEP is a majority-minority institution, the model began as a means of involving Hispanic students; however, its creators soon realized that the model could benefit a broader range of students—with varied educational levels, backgrounds, and experiences. By including diverse student researchers, they would be enhancing the levels of scholarship and research productivity and providing a cross section of perspectives critical to any technical or scientific discipline. As Dr. William Wulf (Wulf, 2006), President of the National Academy of Engineering, stated

> To the extent that engineering lacks diversity, it is impoverished. It is not able to engineer as well as it could. Since the products and processes we create are limited by the life experiences of the workforce, the best solution, the elegant solution, may never be considered because of that lack!

An Integrated Research Environment

Students involved in research develop skills beyond those typically learned in the classroom. They can refine their cognitive and interpersonal skills, enhance their personal growth, and incorporate sound intellectual and management habits. Traditionally, however, only the best and brightest students have enjoyed these benefits. The ARG model adds to the mix students who are competent, but may lack confidence.

Most models focus on a one-on-one student-mentor relationship. With the ARG model, in contrast, a collective of diverse students and faculty mentors contribute to the research effort. In such an integrated environment, faculty mentors are free to create and sustain a cooperative effort targeted at giving students the skills to be successful in research, academia, and the workforce. Students—particularly those from underrepresented groups—and faculty mentors have the opportunity to increase productivity and achieve more. As a result, students are more likely to persist through their undergraduate years and continue to graduate study.

Universal Benefits

Initially, the ARG model targeted underrepresented groups in only the computing areas; however, the impact of the model on other student groups became clear at a 2003 workshop at a university with a vastly different student population. Faculty and student feedback made it clear that the students benefited from the interactions and activities espoused by the model. Any program, regardless of discipline, can adopt the model to help students transition to graduate school or the workplace. The emphasis on cooperative team and leadership skills provides the skills any student needs to have a positive impact on society.

Using This Guide

To realize the full benefits of developing enthusiastic and productive students who work as a research team, the ARG model requires time and resources from both faculty mentors and students. Although intended for faculty mentors, the handbook can be a resource for all group members and is suitable for both newly formed and established research groups. While it is important to embrace the philosophy underlying the ARG model, the guidelines for structuring and maintaining research groups are flexible and adaptable. Groups differ in environments, research areas, and audiences, so each group should feel free to adapt the structure and activities suggested to suit its particular purpose and personality. To successfully implement the model, a group need not include all components or activities. Rather, we offer a compendium of effective undergraduate research practices refined to suit any ARG's development and management.

An Affinity Research Group is first and foremost a team effort in which faculty mentors and students enjoy an environment designed expressly to let each member flourish.

At the heart of the ARG model is the deliberate development of skills that, when applied, result in a highly effective team with common goals. Consequently, the ARG model can benefit groups in which the effort centers around activities such as outreach, service, or peer mentoring—not just research.

A Content Overview

Most of this handbook contains general information about the ARG model and how to design, form, and maintain an ARG. Throughout the main text are small sidebars that relate anecdotes and offer additional insight into adapting the model. The handbook also offers sample activities, templates, and forms that support the group's operation.Chapters 1 and 2 look at the model's foundations—the driving ideology and key elements—and theoretical underpinnings. Chapter 3 delves into the model's structure and examines activities that help develop skills. Chapter 4 focuses on the ARG orientation, which is the single most important tool for establishing healthy norms and infusing the research group with genuine ARG characteristics. Chapter 5 is devoted to issues of managing an ARG, including the challenges and responsibilities of an ARG faculty mentor. Chapter 6 gives guidelines for structured activities that can further a group's research goals and help develop students. Finally, Chapter 7 deals with evaluation and assessment, including an approach to data collection, and presents guidelines on designing and implementing effective assessments. The appendices contain numerous templates, guidelines, sample forms, and other tools.

Acknowledgments

The ARG model was developed at the University of Texas at El Paso through NSF funding from its Minority Institutions Infrastructure (MII) program (grant CDA-9522207) and the U.S. Department of Energy (grant 3-49811). Andy Bernat, Ann Gates, Sergio Cabrera, and Connie Della-Piana conceived and initially implemented the model. Patricia Teller joined the project later and made important contributions to the model. Ann Gates, Steve Roach, Elsa Villa, Gabriel Della-Piana, and Kerrie Kephart have refined and disseminated the model through funding from NSF's Course, Curriculum, and Laboratory Instruction (CCLI) program (grant no. DUE-0443061); dissemination of the ARG model is partially funded by NSF Broadening Participation in Computing grant no. CNS-05405092 and the IEEE New Initiatives program. Those who adopted the ARG model have given useful feedback: Vladik Kreinovich, Olga Kosheleva, Luc Longpré, Patricia Nava, Clint Jeffery, Monica Brockmeyer, and others. We thank the CCLI advisory team in particular for their valuable input: Karl Smith, Jill Singer, Robert Reed, Wendy Carmody, and Ramon Lopez. A special thanks to Nancy Talbert, the handbook copy editor; Mary Contreras and Sue Ann Walker, the project coordinators; and to all the students who participated in research groups over the years, especially Nelly Delgado, Veronica Medina, and Marcus Valenzuela, who assisted in documentation.

Any opinions, findings, and conclusions or recommendations expressed in the handbook are those of the authors and do not necessarily reflect the view of the NSF.

CHAPTER 1: WHAT IS AN AFFINITY RESEARCH GROUP?

An Affinity Research Group (ARG) is, principally, a team effort in which faculty mentors, undergraduates, and graduates enjoy an environment designed expressly to let each member flourish. It is so called because members have or are developing an affinity for the particular research topic. Group members share, to greater or lesser extents, research goals, as well as goals for academic and professional development. This affinity is the basis for promoting cooperation in achieving goals. Members value the contributions of all other members and perceive that their individual contributions are essential to the group's success. "Group success" is thus defined as reaching a set of goals upon which everyone in the group has agreed. Student members generally have varied expertise, capabilities, interests and skills, and educational, cultural, and familial backgrounds. The result is a much richer dialogue about the research problems and their solutions.

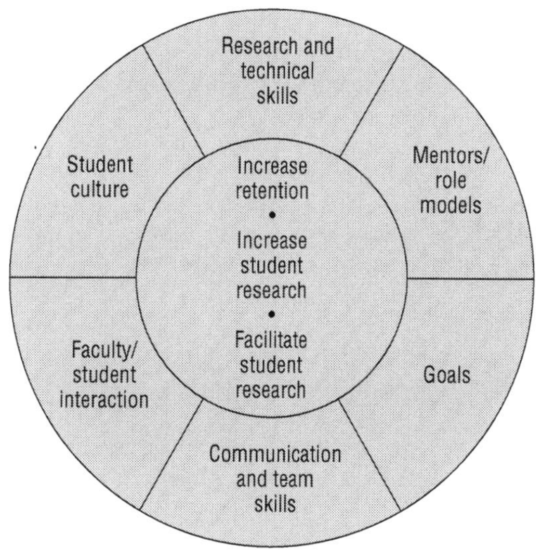

Fig. 1-1: The Affinity Research Group elements.

Fig. 1-1 shows the main elements for ARG. The elements along the outer circle denote the activities that contribute to student retention and success (Rodriguez, 1994): develop a student culture, provide opportunities for student and faculty interaction outside the classroom, provide mentors and role models for students, and assist students in setting clear and attainable goals. The elements at the top and bottom of the outer circle represent the skills (research, technical, communication, and team skills) that lead to the benefits in the inner circle: retention of students, increased involvement of students in research, and overall student success.

Table 1-1. Components of an Affinity Research Group.

Group Component	Faculty Mentor Perspective	Student Perspective
Core Purpose		
	Drives the group's planning and decision-making.	Provides the group with direction, guidance, and inspiration.
Student Connectedness		
Orientation	Helps me... assimilate new members and reinvigorate established ones, provide a forum for voicing concerns and understanding student perspectives, and develop student advocacy for increasing numbers in targeted discipline.	Helps me... deepen my understanding of the ARG model, voice concerns and understand faculty mentor's perspective, and realize the importance of increasing the number of qualified people working in science, math, engineering, and technology fields.
Research project definition	Helps me... align tasks to mission and goals, ensure that we have a work breakdown that will let us achieve our goals, and identify and mitigate risks.	Helps me... understand my contribution as it relates to the whole project and connect to the research project.
Management Scheme		
Define dependencies and timelines	Helps me... understand the steps for completing the research or project, identify the project's critical path and possible risks, and structure individual accountability.	Helps me... understand the importance of tasks and their interdependencies and realize the importance of making progress on defined tasks.
Defined deliverables	Helps me... enforce individual accountability and document results.	Helps me... contribute to the project and practice communication skills.
Meetings and activities —Subgroup meetings	Provides a way to... share research progress and results, identify research problems and brainstorm solutions, develop students' skills and research background, and model professional skills.	Provides a way to... solve problems, practice skills, including developing domain expertise, contribute to the research effort, and exercise cooperative team skills.
—Group meetings	Provides a way to... develop and refine research skills, share information, and practice professional skills.	Provides a way to... report our group's results and learn about work in other subgroups.
—Activities	Provides a way to... advance research findings and students' skills, practice cooperative team and professional skills, and build student confidence and competence.	Provides a way to... develop domain expertise, practice skills, and refine and advance the research agenda.
Process improvement	A means of assessing and evaluating progress of the project, students, and subgroups.	A means of self-assessing progress and subgroup interaction.

Table 1-2. How the ARG model differs from a traditional hierarchical model.

Affinity Research Group Model	Traditional Hierarchical Research Models
Members are concerned about the progress of the team's project.	Members are often concerned about the progress of their individual project.
Heterogeneous membership is encouraged, and undergraduate students are recruited.	Only the best and brightest are recruited, and undergraduate students are rarely included.
Group members share leadership in executing various tasks.	The professor and PhD students exclusively lead the group.
Research, technical, team, and professional skills are emphasized and explicitly taught.	"Necessary" research and technical skills are taught.
Professional skills are developed through structured activities.	Professional skills are assumed.
Cooperative environment is a key part of the model and is encouraged and developed.	Environment is controlled by the research leader and may be competitive.
Process improvement is part of model.	Process improvement is not practiced or is ad hoc.

Affinity Research Group Components

Table 1-1 summarizes the ARG's components and the benefits of incorporating those components from both the faculty mentor and student perspectives. Subsequent chapters cover each component in detail.

As Table 1-2 shows, the ARG model is unique because it deliberately develops the knowledge and skills required for research and cooperative work. The model integrates best practices from a variety of sources in industry, research, and education.

Research group structures are traditionally hierarchical, based on a pyramid structure in which layers represent a decreasing order of expertise and authority. The ARG model incorporates aspects of the traditional model, but it differs sharply in one important aspect: Group members have a peer-to-peer relationship. A faculty mentor still holds a leadership position and provides direction to the other group members, but in the ARG, all student members work together as equals, and each student acquires the skills to be a leader and expert in some aspect of the research that the group is doing as a whole.

Another significant difference is that hierarchical research groups typically are comprised of graduate students whom faculty mentors assume are ready to make meaningful contributions to research without much additional training. The individual's success is correlated to how high in the pyramid he or she rises, sometimes resulting in competition among group members. The competitive nature of this type of group can create an environment that undermines some students' self-confidence and erodes their willingness to contribute (Deutsch, 1949). This effect can be magnified in disciplines already low in participation from underrepresented groups (NSF, 2004a and 2004b).

The cooperative structure of the ARG model allows students with varying skill levels, backgrounds, and experience to flourish because it encourages access to such students. Because its infrastructure provides them with active mentoring and training in research, the model encourages and nurtures participation from a wider range of students.

Using structured tasks and activities, students

- develop domain expertise,
- understand and appreciate the research process and its practice, and
- acquire team, communication, problem-solving, and higher-level thinking skills that will make them effective leaders and successful in research, academia, and industry.

The model has demonstrated success in increasing both the quality of undergraduate students and their participation in advanced studies (Kephart et al., 2008). It began as a way to retain underrepresented groups, such as female students, in computing areas, but we have since refined it to be suitable for a variety of undergraduate groups. The ARG model embraces diversity and exposes all students in the group to a wide range of experiences that will help them develop and transfer knowledge and skills within the research environment. It provides a structure for students

What Influences Success?

When 50 low-income Hispanic students were asked what influenced their academic success in higher education (Gandara, 1995), three-fourths rated persistence as the single most important characteristic rather than ability or intelligence. According to another study (Rodriguez, 1994), the following actions lead to persistence in school:

- engage students as role models for one another,
- provide opportunities for faculty and students to interact outside the classroom,
- foster a "student culture" in which students can interact with one another and discuss issues in a competent manner,
- help students clarify and maintain goals, and
- involve students in their college learning experience because the greater the degree of involvement, the more likely the student will persist to graduation.

Students learn by becoming involved, and success in learning leads to improved retention of students. It is clear that isolation and alienation are the best predictors of failure. According to Rodriguez, students in science, engineering, and math recognized the importance of setting clear personal goals, and those who did not persist indicated confusion and instability as contributing to their decision to leave these fields. This finding is consistent with McLeod (1987).

These and other studies (Astin, 1985; Tinto et al., 1993) served as a guide for developing the ARG model. An ARG provides an atmosphere in which students can become involved and serve as role models for one another. Modeling is the principal means of developing a self-belief of efficacy—the strength and determination to persevere in the face of obstacles and sometimes even rejection (Bandura, 1990). A person's self-worth is raised when a representative of his or her group succeeds by sustained effort. The groups also provide a platform for students to set and assess personal and group goals throughout their education.

to learn, use and integrate technical, communication, and professional skills in a deliberate rather than an ad hoc manner. The model is built on the principle of consciously developing and training researchers in a cooperative environment. The idea is to maximize each student's potential while advancing the organization and operation of research by a diverse set of students. In short, an ARG seeks to maximize each student's ability to reach his or her potential. That is the philosophy behind the ARG model. A guiding principle is to include students who normally would not be involved in research, which is imperative for diversifying the graduate student population and leadership, as well as the technical workforce overall.

Integrating the teaching and practice of professional skills (communication, research, technical, and cooperative team skills) and structuring them into the routine functioning of the group empowers students to transfer the learned skills from their research group to the workplace and graduate school. This philosophy is the force behind the research group, and it is essential that everyone understand and embrace it.

Five Basic Elements

Five basic elements must be present for a group to truly function cooperatively:

- positive interdependence,
- face-to-face promotive interaction,
- individual and group accountability,
- professional skills, and
- group processing.

Five Elements of Cooperation

As we noted earlier, cooperation and mutual respect are at the core of the ARG model (Johnson et al, 1989, 1990, 1991, 1992a, 1992b). The mere formation of a group does not ensure that it will function cooperatively. As David Johnson and colleagues (1990, p. 4) note,

> Cooperation is working together to accomplish shared goals. Within cooperative activities, individuals seek outcomes that are beneficial to themselves and beneficial to all other group members.

In an ARG, group members work together to maximize their own and others' productivity and achievement. Cooperative groups create better quality products, achieve mastery or competence of a task, develop a social network, and increase group members' self-esteem.

The ARG model ensures that structured cooperative learning techniques are part of the group's routine functioning. Because teaching and practicing professional skills are part of the research group activities, for example, students are able to learn skills from their groups and transfer them to other environments.

Five basic elements must be present for the group to truly function cooperatively: positive interdependence, face-to-face promotive interaction, individual and group accountability, professional skills, and group processing. The ARG model incorporates all five by structuring them into weekly activities and in the group's day-to-day functioning as long as it exists. Chapter 3 describes how these cooperative elements link to the ARG's functions.

Impact of Positive Interdependence and Promotive Interaction

When Fred presented his thesis to us – and this was not anything any faculty said we should do – he just did, and then we asked him questions. And when Martha got her PhD, we did the same thing for her. I did my thesis and they did the same thing for me… I guess that just illustrates the culture of the group: "I want to do this for you, and you'll do it for me when I'm there." And so that's why they showed up on a Saturday afternoon. Not because they didn't have anything better to do, but because I asked them to.
(Former ARG member)

Positive Interdependence

By deliberately structuring groups, we can create an environment where the positive interdependence among group members thrives. In this environment, each group member has a personal stake in the group's success and believes that the group values his or her contributions. Everyone recognizes that all team members bring special skills and abilities that are essential to the project's success.

Positive interdependence can be structured into the research group by assigning roles, setting common goals, or sharing resources. For example, everyone might participate in deciding on a name for their project, defining or refining the group's mission, or creating a group website.

Face-to-face Promotive Interaction

All group members should feel comfortable exchanging and sharing ideas and resources. The explicit goal in this sharing process is for members to help one another succeed and, therefore, help the group reach its goals. It is important to acknowledge and recognize each member's contribution, and a key skill is to constructively critique ideas, not people. The practice of constructive critique is essential to the improvement of both individuals and the group.

Faculty mentors can structure face-to-face promotive interaction by recognizing students' accomplishments at a monthly meeting, celebrating birthdays, publicly acknowledging the group or a person for a job well done, and having group members thank one another for a successful meeting. At the end of the meeting, the group leader might actually say, "Please turn to your neighbors and thank them for their contributions."

Individual and Group Accountability

Each person must be responsible for tangibly contributing his or her fair share to the group. Likewise, the group as a whole is responsible for the group's smooth function and for delivering the required work.

Individual accountability is critical for developing a strong individual. With accountability structured into the group, students can make self-assessments about their deficiencies and weaknesses and seek help to improve. Strategies for structuring individual and group accountability include

- asking students to explain an aspect of the group's effort,
- impromptu questioning in the student's area of study,
- calling on the student to explain his or her research, and
- assigning distinct tasks to students along with deliverables.

Constructing timelines (Gantt charts) and explicitly showing the dependencies among individual and group tasks (Pert charts) are other effective techniques for structuring individual and group accountability.

Professional Skills

In the ARG, professional skills are explicitly taught and practiced in activities designed around one or more technical topics, such as discussing a paper or critiquing a presentation. Professional skills can be anything from active listening and participation to summarizing, providing directions, synthesizing ideas, asking questions, and constructively critiquing. Fomenting effective professional skills makes for more productive and successful interaction among group members and is key to maintaining positive interdependence.

Faculty mentors must not assume that students come with the necessary skills to work in groups. It is not sufficient to simply put students together in a group setting and assume that they will learn to work effectively together. Imagine a group of basketball players who are proficient at the skills of passing and shooting, but have never played on a team. It is not realistic to expect them to win against a team that has been training with a coach.

One way to learn the group skills is to describe the audio and visual cues of someone practicing a particular skill. For example, to emphasize group participation in the completion of a task, the faculty mentor might structure an activity at a meeting and explicitly assign the gatekeeper role (see "Roles to Support a Professional Environment"). Before students begin the activity, they would review the types of behaviors a gatekeeper would have, such as turning to look at someone, asking someone what he or she thinks about the problem, and suggesting to the team that they haven't heard from one of the members recently. In addition to having activities that let students deliberately practice these skills, the faculty mentor might model the behaviors during meetings. Over time, with repeated exposure, everyone will begin to automatically incorporate appropriate behaviors.

Group Processing

As part of the ARG model, faculty mentors and other group members regularly reflect on how well they are achieving their goals and how well their group is functioning. After reviewing results, the faculty mentors determine how the program needs to change, and group members meet to determine how their group must change to improve.

Because the group has dynamic membership, each group must take care to continually reflect on its functioning and adjust its functions as necessary. A group

Roles to Support a Professional Environment

In *The Nuts and Bolts of Cooperative Learning*, David Johnson and colleagues (1994) list roles that support a cooperative, professional environment.

Roles that support group functioning

- **Explainer of ideas or procedures.** Shares ideas and opinions.
- **Recorder.** Writes down the group's decisions and edits the group's report.
- **Gatekeeper.** Ensures that all members are contributing and gives both verbal and nonverbal support and acceptance by seeking and praising others' ideas and conclusions.
- **Direction giver.** Gives direction to the group's work by reviewing the instructions and restating the task's purpose, by calling attention to the time limits, and by offering procedures on how to complete the task most effectively.
- **Clarifier/Paraphraser.** Restates what other members have said to understand or clarify a message.

Roles that help the team formulate information

- **Summarizer.** Restates the group's major conclusions or answers as completely and accurately as possible without referring to notes or to the original material.
- **Accuracy coach.** Corrects any mistakes in another member's explanations or summaries and adds important information that was left out.
- **Understanding checker.** Ensures that all group members can explain how to arrive at an answer or conclusion.
- **Elaborator.** Relates concepts and strategies to other material and existing cognitive frameworks
- **Perspective-taking roles (for each member).** Contributes a perspective or viewpoint to the group's final product.

Roles that help the team ferment ideas and resolve conflict

- **Idea criticizer.** Intellectually challenges group members by criticizing their ideas while communicating respect for them as individuals.
- **Justification asker.** Asks members to give the facts and reasoning that justify their conclusions and answers.
- **Differentiator.** Differentiates the ideas and reasoning of group members so that everyone understands the differences in members' conclusions and reasoning.
- **Integrator.** Integrates members' ideas and reasoning into a single position that everyone can agree on.
- **Extender.** Extends members' ideas and conclusions by adding information or implications.
- **Prober.** Asks in-depth questions that lead to analysis or deeper understanding.

tends to this task by scheduling a regular time when all group members reflect on what is working well, what is not, and what can be done to improve.

Incorporating these cooperative elements might require a steady, incremental approach in which the group adopts structuring techniques only in so far as its comfort level allows. Through reflection, assessment, and further study, such as attending one of the many available professional development workshops in cooperative learning (www.co-operation.org), faculty mentors can deepen their understanding of the ARG model, which in turn will allow them to integrate more cooperative elements into the group's activities.

CHAPTER 2: THEORY BEHIND THE MODEL

One can draw from two social psychological theories to frame our understanding of how ARGs operate, and why they could be used to successfully develop the domain knowledge, professional skills, and research abilities of a broad range of students. The theory behind cooperative learning explains how the deliberate design of social structures can create an environment in which ARG members flourish because each member perceives that his or her contributions are essential to reaching the group's goal. In addition, each group member values the contributions of all other members and perceives that each member's contributions are valued.

When such positive interdependence and a sense of shared goals develops among group members, over time the possibility for an ARG to become a "community of practice" arises. Communities of practice (Lave and Wenger, 1991; Lave and Wenger, 1999) are social spaces that promote deep learning through interaction among novice and more expert group members.

Affinity as a Transformative Experience

I was pretty individualistic, wanted to study on my own and was being forced to work together, work with other people...And [we were] learning about cooperative learning. Not just 'here's the theory,' but we were seeing it work in practice.
(Former ARG member)

Cooperative Learning

In the previous chapter, we outlined the ARG's cooperative learning framework. The structure of cooperative learning, on which the framework depends, comes from three broad theoretical perspectives: social interdependence, socio-cognitive development, and behaviorism. Of these, the theory of social interdependence (Johnson et al., 1989) is what explains how interaction differences within groups will lead to different outcomes.

Social interdependence theory says that the structure of interaction will determine whether positive, negative, or no interdependence results, and this in turn will affect group and individual outcomes. Positive, or cooperative, interdependence occurs when two or more people interact in ways to promote one another's success. When positive interdependence is present, members perceive that they have attained their goals only if the others have also attained theirs. Negative, or competitive, interdependence occurs when two or more people interact in ways to obstruct the success of others. Negative interdependent situations are win-lose because an individual achieves personal goals at the expense of others. In individual endeavors, obviously, no interdependence exists, and the individual is solely responsible for his or her rise or fall.

The outcomes of cooperation or promotive interaction typically benefit both individual and group: positive relationships, greater effort to achieve, and psychological adjustment or social competence. The ARG model strives to structure group interactions in a way that fosters positive interdependence and promotive interaction, generally yielding the following outcomes:

Value of Participation in a Community of Practice

I was a freshman and Martha was a senior. And one day I was walking in the hall and Martha was like, "you're coming to the ACM meeting." And I had never been to an ACM meeting, didn't know what it was all about, and so just having someone senior say, "Hey, why don't you come with me?" ...I don't think I would've gone in on my own or become involved in ACM on my own, but it was the encouragement from somebody I respected. (Former ARG member)

- establishment and maintenance of cooperative groups and subgroups,
- achievement of research deliverables; and
- self-development of group members, who acquire teaming and research skills and progress in cognitive and emotional development.

These defining characteristics distinguish ARGs from more traditional, hierarchical research groups.

Situated Learning

An essential facet of the ARG model is the idea that groups form around goals that all members share and that newer members learn by participating in research activities under the guidance of more experienced members. Learning is "situated" because it takes place in a community of practice, a social space conducive to deep learning and disciplinary socialization. Examples other than an ARG might be anything from a grade school classroom to a craft guild or professional academic association. For anthropologist Jean Lave and computer scientist Etienne Wenger, the theory's creators, learning is situated in certain forms of social participation, and is distributed among co-participants in a community of practice. Situated learning runs counter to the traditional view of learning as an individualistic and mental phenomenon.

The ARG model embodies several aspects of situated learning. One, as mentioned earlier, is the notion of situatedness, where learning occurs when students engage in authentic, meaningful, real-world practices. When teaching is not situated in direct, meaningful experience, people have more difficulty making sense of what they are learning, turning new experience into abstract ideas, and therefore, in transferring material to new situations.

The community of practice notion also connects with the ARG model. The idea is that some underlying social purpose exists for a group's activities that serves to motivate participation by community (group) members. Over time, the purpose organizes the group's activities into a body of practice. In communities of practice as Lave and Wenger envision them, learning is like an apprenticeship; indeed, the authors draw on craft apprenticeship to illuminate some key concepts related to the model. More experienced community members carry more responsibility and are expected to perform at higher levels of expertise than novice members. And, as in an apprenticeship, novice members learn by participating alongside more experienced members, first from the periphery of the group's core activities and then gradually by taking on greater responsibility as their knowledge and expertise develops.

Lave and Wenger view the novice's participation in the community of practice as both legitimate and peripheral.

The participation is legitimate because novices participate in a way that is engaged and recognized as important to the group's goals. It is also peripheral because a novice's participation typically requires less knowledge and skills and perhaps a lower commitment to the group's core purpose.

Although newcomers might participate only in a limited way in the group's activities, they are not disconnected from the group's primary practices. Rather, the idea of peripherality "suggests an opening, a way of gaining access to sources for understanding through growing involvement" (Lave and Wenger, 1999, p. 87). Without such an opening and the support provided by more experienced ARG members, novice students might not have access to the skills, abilities, and knowledge that lead to fuller participation in a field of study. For ARG members, fuller participation might mean enrolling in and completing graduate school. Thus, it is through the intentional design of ARGs, using principles of cooperative learning, that communities of practice are fostered. Novice undergraduate students are recruited into research groups, participating as legitimate, peripheral members alongside graduate students and faculty mentors in a cooperative research group. They gradually gain in expertise while developing an authentic vision of themselves as researchers.

Independent Learning: Does It Really Exist?

Situated learning asserts that learning does not occur in a vacuum. Even people who are adept at book learning and may appear to be self-taught are always drawing on the experiences and insights of others, encapsulated in texts and other media. More often than not, such seemingly independent learners are also immersed in environments that support their ability to make sense of what they are learning "on their own."

CHAPTER 3: FIRST STEPS

The principal reason for an ARG is to create a cooperative environment in which students with different abilities can succeed in research or other important tasks. Consequently, cooperation is key to structuring such a group, which consists of three steps:

1. Define the group's core purpose.
2. Promote student connections.
3. Apply effective management practices, including practices that reinforce skills development and promote the establishment of cooperative teams.

Define a Core Purpose

All ARGs must have both a core purpose and core values. The core purpose is why the group exists, beyond simply "to reach research project goals." As Jim Collins and Jerry Porras note in *Built to Last: Successful Habits of Visionary Companies* (1994), the core purpose guides and inspires all group members and remains relatively fixed in time. Some large ARGs might work on numerous research projects—all driven by a single core purpose. As projects are completed and new ones started, the core purpose remains constant.

The core purpose sets the stage for defining core values—a set of three to six simply stated principles that guide the group's actions. For example, the stated core values of Nordstrom's department store include the following: service to the customer above all else, hard work and productivity, continuous improvement, and never being satisfied.

As the sidebar "Two Years Later" describes, defining the core purpose can take many months (but, one hopes, not years). It might be a purpose your group is passionate about or one that is central to the clients you serve, or your product, or an innovation, or none of these. The following questions can help a group determine the validity of a core purpose:

- Is it authentic?
- Does the ideology it represents characterize the group's culture?
- Do all group leaders believe it?
- Do your actions align with the ideology?
- Can group members articulate the ideology at any given time?
- Does the ideology guide decision-making?

If the answer is "yes" to all these questions, the group's core purpose has been determined. A group united and driven by a core purpose is likely to be more productive and stable, and its members will have more cohesion and synergy.

ARG Core Values

The ARG model espouses three core values:

- **Student Success.** An ARG values the deliberate development of skills in each student to ensure his or her success.
- **Cooperation.** An ARG values cooperation in all interactions, including mutual respect of opinions and ideas of all the members, promotive interaction, positive interdependence, and individual accountability.
- **Excellence.** An ARG values excellence and strives to achieve it in all its actions.

Two Years Later

I did not fully appreciate the difficulty of defining the core purpose until I tried to articulate one for a research group that Steve Roach and I oversaw. I was talking with Dr. Jerry Porras, a coauthor with Dr. Jim Collins of *Built to Last*, about what characterizes companies that have endured for at least a century. One common element was the definition of a core purpose, which the companies used to drive their decision making. That fundamental starting point captured the notion of why companies did what they did. So Porras asked me, "What is your research group's core purpose?"

I immediately said, "To advance the state-of-the-art in software engineering." To my surprise, he responded, "I don't believe that's true! If it were, you would belong to an institution that concerns itself solely with research and nothing else." He went on to ask me more questions, and for every response I gave, he continued to ask, "Why?"

Several weeks later, I continued the conversation with my colleague, Steve. He and I had numerous discussions about our research group's core purpose. After two years, we finally agreed that the following statement captures why we do what we do: "To develop students with diverse backgrounds by involving them in research that contributes to society."

Finally, we had captured the true reason for choosing our particular projects and the students who work with us.

—Ann Gates, PhD

As its name implies, a core purpose preserves the group's core (Collins and Porras, 1994). Because all members need to believe in it, the group must have some way to inculcate the purpose on new members and renew it for existing ones. In the ARG model, the orientation serves this function; however, any mechanism will suffice that embeds the core purpose and values in all group activities and allows all members to review this core ideology.

Promote Student Connections

Evaluations early in the development of the ARG model revealed that students and faculty mentors perceived the students' assigned tasks quite differently (Gates et al., 1999a). Undergraduates did not understand the significance of their assigned tasks, their group's goals and organization, or how their individual assigned tasks fit with those goals. They often concluded that tasks were "busy work," and thus of no consequence. Further analysis of how faculty mentors assigned tasks revealed a lack of clear communication about the project's goals and motivation and about how the tasks work together to reach project goals.

The analysis revealed that it is not enough simply to discuss goals and tasks and have students read about the project. Rather, to establish a clear connection between assigned tasks and the project, faculty mentors must provide students with a succinct description of the research goals and the significance of each to the project. The description should also identify any task interdependencies. By making this information available to everyone in the group—in a directory, on a website, or as part of a project management system—everyone can see clearly how individual tasks contribute to the project's and group's overall success.

The ARG model is designed to promote this connectedness through mechanisms such as the annual orientation and management practices. The annual orientation, which Chapter 4 describes in detail, helps assimilate new students into the research group, provides members with an understanding of basic group and research skills, and reveals student and faculty concerns. The orientation represents an important opportunity for both faculty mentors and students. It helps faculty mentors in communicating research group structure and behaviors, and both faculty and students can use it to assess and evaluate the model in light of the group composition, project demands, and students' attitudes.

Apply Effective Management Practices

The last focal point in structuring an ARG is to use management best practices, including but not limited to defining dependencies, timelines, and deliverables; scheduling meetings and activities; and supporting continuous

I'm Not Sure I Know Enough

Like many faculty members, I assign complex problems to my students. Shortly after I had given a particularly challenging problem to my junior class, I happened to be leaving the building late, so I peeked into the lab to see who was there. Three of my better students from the junior class were listening as a fourth student—Mary— explained the problem's solution. As the three continued questioning her, she patiently explained clearly and precisely the key points of the solution that I had hoped they would discover. I was mildly surprised, since Mary had not stood out in class. A few weeks later, one of the midterm exam questions was related to that problem, and each of the three students answered correctly. To my surprise, Mary's answer was weak, as was the rest of her exam. When I asked her privately how she could teach others but not answer the question herself, she made no excuses. She was working full time off campus and didn't have the chance to review before the midterm. More important, whenever she had to explain things in writing, she took a very long time because she didn't think her written English was adequate.

I continued to observe that Mary was clearly able to explain the course concepts and to write programs to solve the problems, but her grades never rose above mediocre. When I had the opportunity, I offered her a job as an undergraduate researcher. Initially, she was delighted, but a few days later stated that she didn't think she could do the work because she didn't know enough to contribute. I assured her that she was the right person for the job.

The research position meant that Mary could spend more time on campus, and her grades improved. She went on to graduate school, completed her Master's degree, and is now a database administrator. She contributed to the group, not only through her research, but also through her assistance to other students in their projects and with her ability to help others collaborate in solving similar problems.

While working as my teaching assistant in a senior course, Mary asked me to consider including a particular student in the research group. I was doubtful. John seemed entirely unmotivated in my class, was barely passing the program, and was in jeopardy of not having the minimum GPA for graduation. However, I trusted Mary enough to look at him more closely. In meetings outside class, I pressed John with open-ended technical questions, and I was soon impressed by how much he knew and how well he could synthesize information to obtain solutions. When I invited him to join the research group, he too was excited, but later doubted his ability to do the work. Again, the reason was his perception that he lacked the knowledge.

As I had done with Mary, I assured him that he was the right person for the job. John stuck with it and applied for graduate studies. At my insistence, the graduate committee accepted him provisionally. In contrast to his undergraduate career, John maintained a perfect 4.0 GPA in graduate school, and his technical expertise and problem-solving abilities became invaluable resources for the research group.

—Steve Roach, PhD

quality improvement. Again, cooperation is paramount. The faculty mentor must realize the importance of consciously structuring the elements of cooperative teams in the manner described in the previous chapter. A research or development team is not a trivial undertaking, as the volumes of how-to research and literature attest. Although Chapter 5 of this handbook does cover project management issues specific to managing an ARG, it is by no means exhaustive.

Joining the Group

An ARG follows the traditional model of a research

group in that a faculty mentor invites the student to join. After that, the two models radically depart. In the traditional model, only the obviously best and brightest students are invited. The ARG, in contrast, is designed to accommodate students with "hidden" talent, those who have the skill but, perhaps, not the confidence and who fail to recognize or appreciate their talent. The sidebar "I'm Not Sure I Know Enough" describes two such cases. In both, the students had the knowledge and the motivation, but it took a sensitive faculty mentor and a sensitive student group member to appreciate that.

Recruiting students into a ARG requires that mentors realize that a lack of self confidence is not necessarily related to a lack of ability. Mentors must be able to recognize and explicitly try to involve students who possess a certain aptitude level, but who lack the self-confidence and self-awareness to recognize or realize their own potential.

These students do not normally self-select and will not volunteer to join the group. As the sidebar shows, they might initially be flattered and responsive to an invitation to join, but they might also turn down such invitations because of their lack of confidence. For students like the two described in the sidebar "I'm Not Sure I Know Enough," the ARG model is of particular benefit because it offers them a chance to get the training they need to overcome their perceived weaknesses and gain confidence and skill to take on progressively greater responsibilities. As their expertise grows and their skill levels are honed through the structured activities, such students become more confident.

CHAPTER 4: THE ORIENTATION

In the ARG model, group membership is dynamic: Members graduate and new students join with different levels of knowledge and skills that grow at different rates. As Chapter 3 describes, one of an ARG's key elements is student connectedness—students must be connected to the group and understand its organization and goals. The orientation (Gates et al., 1999b; Teller and Gates, 2001), usually scheduled at the beginning of the school year, provides students with the opportunity to achieve both requirements. Depending on the objectives of the orientation, it can take from 4 to 8 hours.

The orientation is a way for new members to

- understand the ARG model's philosophy and goals, the research goals of the projects to which they are assigned, and the basic elements of the research process, and
- learn the basis of the cooperative paradigm described in the first chapter, become aware of faculty mentors' expectations, and understand the resources available to them.

The orientation is a way for established members to

- renew their commitment to the group,
- improve their research and professional skills, and
- enhance the group learning process with the goal of improving the group's effectiveness.

Finally, the orientation is a way for faculty mentors to

- become aware of members' misgivings and expectations of the ARG experience, and
- process among themselves to reevaluate the model and its success.

Orientations are not typical in university research environments, but without an orientation, assimilating new members into a research group can be time-consuming for both students and faculty mentors. This is particularly true

An ARG orientation is geared to facilitate new students and to increase ownership of the model.

for groups that include students who may lack confidence and preparedness and groups that are based on a structure that is cooperative rather than hierarchical. Like the ARG's day-to-day activities, the orientation's structure is built on the use of cooperative learning techniques, which further promote cooperative skills.

> **Why an Orientation?**
>
> The orientation helps students
>
> - understand basic group and research skills and
> - define research goals for the year.
>
> It helps faculty mentors reevaluate the functioning of their research groups.

Preparation

The ARG's cooperative nature is reflected in the orientation preparation. Student facilitators, who are established group members, assist faculty mentors and are given the opportunity to gain ownership of the ARG and further develop their professional skills. More important, they have a chance to facilitate a cooperative meeting and apply what they have learned. Faculty planning meetings are effective ways to define the orientation's general outline and to assign tasks to each faculty mentor, giving one faculty mentor the responsibility of designing and developing each orientation component. A session template can aid in defining the essential component elements (goal, objectives, duration, and materials) and activities. Before the orientation, the mentors decide what methods to use in forming groups and delivering component activities. Documentation, including an agenda, is required. A sample agenda appears in Appendix D, pp. 88.

Foundational Elements

As the diagram in Figure 4-1 shows, the orientation covers student and faculty introductions, ARG philosophy and goals, cooperative group skills, research activities and skills, and competing concerns. Each of these five components achieves its main objectives through carefully designed activities that promote the actions on the circle's rim: achieve, learn, own, understand, renew, and involve. The teaching and practice of professional skills is a secondary objective in each component.

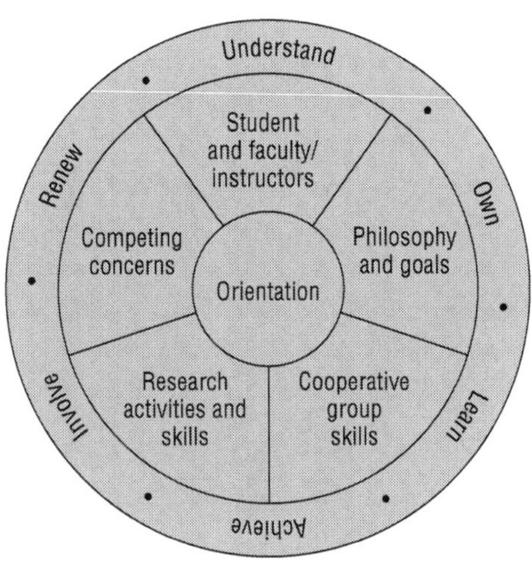

Figure 4-1: Components of a successful ARG orientation.

Cooperative groups are a cornerstone of orientation, and each student must be able to articulate the answers of other group members. The group's composition depends on the activity's objective. At any time, facilitators might assign such roles as gatekeeper, summarizer, timekeeper, recorder, paraphraser, direction giver, and initiator. (The Chapter 1 sidebar "Roles to Support a Professional Environment" briefly describes these roles.) After assigning the appropriate roles, the faculty mentor makes the role behaviors explicit by describing the physical and verbal actions associated with roles (Johnson et al., 1989). When discussing the timekeeper role, for example, the facilitator might ask the group to describe what a person observing a timekeeper would see or hear. The group might reply with what the timekeeper could say, such as, "We need to move on," "We're running out of time," or "Let's get back to our task." A physical cue could be looking at or pointing to your watch. Making the behaviors expected of each role explicit might seem unnecessary, but it is an effective way to teach and learn basic professional skills. Furthermore, role assignments allow a shy or normally reserved students "permission" to participate. It says to the student, "you cannot just quietly do your job: I expect to see and hear you." This distinction is important, particularly when the student lacks confidence or the culture inhibits direct participation.

Student and Faculty Introductions

The orientation officially begins with student and faculty introductions, which have two objectives:

1. Assimilate new members into the group.
2. Motivate the rest of the orientation.

In a larger sense, the objective is to establish familiarity among participants. People come to ARGs with varying levels of skills and confidence, and some are reluctant to introduce themselves. For these reasons, it is essential to have some ice-breaking activity. At UTEP, students acquaint themselves with three unfamiliar people, using information on name tags as conversation catalysts. Techniques for doing this vary, but a popular one is to find two people in the room who have provided answers similar to one's own name-tag questions. For example, if a name-tag question is "What is your favorite food," the students would be asked to find three people in the room who listed the same kind of food. The idea is to learn something about the people in the room. This type of ice-breaker works particularly well if time is short, and even students who already know one another have fun with it.

If more time is available, the ice-breaker can involve more in-depth questions with heterogeneous groups comprising undergraduates and graduates, new members and previous members, and even a mix of faculty and students. The groups might share answers to questions such as, "How do you rate your university experience on a scale from 1 to 10 and why?" or "What person most influenced your decision to go to college?" or "How did you choose your major?"

To enhance familiarity among groups, introductions typically move from discussion within a group to interaction among groups. Faculty and student facilitators monitor the groups and encourage members to elaborate on their answers to the earlier questions. The idea is to highlight the variety that occurs when more groups are involved.

Thus, in meeting the first objective of this orientation component—assimilate new members—activities establish base groups. These are randomly assigned groups to which students return at different times during the orientation or even throughout the year. Given enough time, base groups provide trusted environments.

Appendix D, p. 92, contains a questionnaire that can help members evaluate how well they contribute to the group. The questionnaire identifies actions that directly contribute to the completion of some task, such as giving or seeking information or options, providing directions, or defining roles. The questionnaire also helps evaluate indirect contributions that maintain the group's effectiveness by facilitating communication or providing encouragement. The degree to which each of these actions is performed indicates the leadership that a student exhibits. The assessment can help faculty track a student's leadership growth through the life of the ARG.

Philosophy and Goals

After student and faculty introductions, the orientation moves to the discussion of the ARG's philosophy and goals, including how groups are organized. At UTEP, new members discuss the low number of students entering science, technology, engineering, and mathematics and try to understand how the ARG model addresses these issues.

The ARG has three main goals:

1. Increase student retention.
2. Increase student research participation.
3. Develop students' expertise and skills to ensure their success.

To educate students about the ARG philosophy and goals, the faculty mentor presents a statement that justifies the ARG goals, such as

> A National Academy of Science survey showed that over 50% of high school seniors surveyed dropped out of the science, engineering and math pipeline by the end of

their first year in college. Some returned later; however, only 35% of high school seniors who planned on degrees in these fields actually obtained them.

Facilitators assign roles, review the behaviors associated with the roles, and pose questions to students in base groups. The questions associated with the earlier sample statement might be as follows:

- What factors contribute to students switching from science, engineering, and math majors?
- What can be done to increase the number of students going to graduate school?

The facilitator rotates roles for each question. After the time period for group discussion ends, a member from each group discusses the group's responses, which the facilitator records on a flip chart. A faculty mentor then relates the discussion to the ARG goals. For the sample statement, the facilitator would emphasize that the ARG model addresses the dropout rate by providing an atmosphere in which students can learn technical, research, communication, and professional skills. The facilitator also explains the model's distinguishing features, such as how it integrates undergraduates and develops skills through cooperative learning. Appendix D, p. 96, includes Boeing's Desired Attributes of an Engineer (Anderson, 1995), which facilitators can use as a basis for identifying valuable professional skills and discussing how the ARG model contributes to the development of these skills in students.

Cooperative Team Skills

The next set of orientation activities addresses how to practice cooperative team skills and structure such skills into day-to-day group functioning. This orientation component has three objectives:

1. Enhance the students' awareness of how they work in groups.
2. Understand what constitutes professionalism.
3. Understand the five basic elements needed to structure cooperative teams: positive interdependence, face-to-face promotive interaction, professional skills development, individual accountability, and group processing.

For the most part, students perform cooperative team skills activities in groups of five. In one activity, the group solves a problem under each of three learning paradigms: individualistic, competitive, and cooperative. For cooperative problem solving, students have assigned roles. The group then discusses how the paradigms differ and the advantages and disadvantages of each. The goal is to underline the usefulness of working collaboratively.

Another activity uses the jigsaw technique, as described in "Sample Agenda For a Four-Hour Orientation," in Appendix D, p. 88. Each member of each group has one of five sections of a handout that discusses the five basic elements of cooperative groups. Students assigned to the same section form their own group to read, discuss, and plan a presentation that includes an example of how the element was modeled during the orientation. Returning to their respective base groups, each student explains that section of the handout. The goal is to demonstrate how to structure cooperation into group activities.

In another activity, often done after the jigsaw exercise, students break into groups of three and use cooperative skills to solve a problem. Facilitators evaluate group interaction with the help of an observation form. At the end of the exercise, the facilitators discuss their observations with the group.

The activities on cooperative team building end with a summary that relates the importance of using cooperative skills in research groups. Each student is given a handout that summarizes the skills and techniques he or she can use to further cooperation in the group.

To address the objective of understanding professionalism, groups may be given scenarios that cover the ethical issues confronting employees, such as honesty, integrity, respect, trust, responsibility, and citizenship. For each scenario, group members must decide what set of actions a person should take. Groups discuss the scenarios, come to consensus on actions, and present their justifications in a discussion that involves all the groups.

The activities with some suggested time limits are described in more detail in the sample orientation in Appendix D, p. 88.

Research Activities and Skills

The next part of the orientation provides students with a framework for understanding how they can contribute to research. Students gain a basic understanding of the research goals, process, and supporting infrastructure.

Activities are divided into two sessions. New members attend only the first session. Heterogeneous groups of new members from the first session and established members attend the second session. Invited faculty mentors can also attend either session to share their ideas.

The first session addresses the research goals and process in a brainstorming session. After facilitators explain brainstorming and pose questions, groups brainstorm for a fixed time. For each question, a facilitator records group responses and then promotes discussion by asking such questions as, "What are the goals of research?" or "What steps does the research process follow?" or "What are the rewards and challenges of doing research?"

In the second session, participants address the supporting research infrastructure by discussing the following project management topics:

- methods for defining the project's mission, goals, and duration,
- contact information for project managers and team members,
- task breakdown,
- task relationships to project goals, associated deliverables, timelines, and
- status reporting.

Because of time constraints, the orientation cannot address such concerns as research topic selection, research methods, literature review and surveys, time management, written and oral presentation skills, proposal preparation, and criteria for reviewing oral presentations and papers. Rather, students are given an information packet with materials on these and related topics, and typically practice these skills and techniques in subsequent small- and large-group meetings.

Competing Concerns

The orientation concludes by exploring the issues and concerns about being a member of the group. These concerns are explored from the perspective of both students and faculty. The aim is to promote communication and professionalism and foster trust among all group members—both faculty and students—by understanding and appreciating each other's concerns. Faculty concerns generally center on student professionalism—can students meet their responsibilities, manage their time, behave proactively, contribute tangibly, and be ethical? Student concerns typically center on meeting mentor expectations, contributing to research, learning the skills needed to succeed in research, and balancing coursework and research.

The main activity for this part of the orientation aims to address immediate concerns. Students and faculty are in separate groups. Using brainstorming (as described in the "Brainstorming" sidebar) students answer, "As a student ARG member, what concerns do you have?" Faculty mentors answer, "As a faculty ARG member, what do you expect from a student member of your group?" After each group comes up with a list, the respective groups prioritize their list. To aid in this activity, Appendix D, p. 94, includes a handout explaining the Nominal Group Technique (NGT), one possible prioritization approach. Faculty mentors then join the students to discuss the concerns that arose from each brainstorming session and

Brainstorming

Goal

To involve all participants in generating a large number of ideas by providing an environment that is free of criticism and judgment, and that encourages the contribution of creative responses.

Process

Assemble the participants into groups of four to seven. The facilitator may allow the participants to self-select, or he or she may create heterogeneous groups based on skill levels, seniority, or other relevant characteristics. The instructions to the groups are as follows:

1. **Set the ground rules.** Emphasize that no comments, either positive or negative, are allowed during the brainstorming session. Any idea, no matter how divergent or seemingly irrelevant, is accepted.
2. **Set the time limit.** A brainstorming session typically lasts approximately 15 to 30 minutes, depending on the size of the group.
3. **State the brainstorming question or problem.** Make sure that the question or problem is stated clearly. Post the question or problem where everyone has access to it, and ensure that everyone understands the task.
4. **Assign a recorder.** The facilitator can use a random technique to select a recorder from each group, or he or she can ask each group to select a recorder. As ideas are generated, the recorder should write each on a flipchart. Remind the group that analysis or evaluation of ideas is not to be done during brainstorming.
5. **Contribute ideas.** Each member contributes one idea by going from one member to another in a systematic way. If a member does not have an idea to contribute, he or she passes. The process continues until no more ideas are generated, or the time limit expires. A less structured approach is to allow anyone to give his or her ideas at any time.
6. **Evaluate the ideas.** The group reviews the ideas for clarity and discards duplicates. If desired, the group could be given three (or more) stickers to place on the top ideas.

how the ARG model can address some of these concerns, particularly those that deal with skills development and time management.

CHAPTER 5: PROJECT MANAGEMENT

Maintaining an ARG has some of the same challenges inherent in any group environment, such as turnover, change, and conflict. To overcome these and ensure that the group continues to function cooperatively and productively, faculty mentors must proactively guide the group's

- focus,
- resource management,
- networking (both internal and external), and
- day-to-day operations, such as project planning.

Although this chapter offers some guidance, more exhaustive sources on effectively managing groups and teams are listed in the sidebar "Project Management Resources." As with any group, dynamics within an ARG occur because of people's natural differences. Consequently, faculty mentors can successfully apply general guidance and principles for group maintenance and troubleshooting. The sidebar contains resources we've found valuable, but the particular source is less important than the idea of adapting the techniques given so that they complement, rather than conflict with, the basic principles of the ARG and cooperative learning models.

In a newly formed affinity group, the faculty mentor takes on the responsibility for project management. As the group matures, students begin to take on more responsibilities with less guidance from the faculty mentor.

In a newly formed affinity group, the faculty mentor takes on the responsibility for project management. As the group matures, students begin to take on more responsibilities with less guidance from the faculty mentor.

Group Focus

To keep students motivated and inspired by their group's core purpose and values, faculty mentors must ensure that the espoused core values are creatively and actively expressed and applied in most facets of the group's life. When students see this, they are more likely to remain committed to the group and, therefore, to its success. Faculty mentors need to pay particular attention to how core values are applied and regularly review and update their application. Although the core values themselves do not change, mentors might need to find ways of making them more tangible to group members.

Project Management Resources

Goodwin, T.K. and E. Hoagland (1999). *How to Get Started in Research* (2nd ed.). Council on Undergraduate Research.

The booklet provides a quick guide for faculty members who are interested in launching an undergraduate research program. It outlines the rationale for including undergraduates in research, tips for selecting students, and the benefits associated with undergraduate research. Issues surrounding space, funding, and equipment are discussed. The authors offer hints for writing successful proposals and Web sites that list grant opportunities.

Hakim, Toufic M. (2000). *How to Develop and Administer Institutional Undergraduate Research Programs*. Washington, D.C.: Council on Undergraduate Research.

Similar in scope to Goodwin and Hoagland (1999) and providing more detailed information, this book includes vignettes to assist the reader in contextualizing the various situations presented. The author also describes the impact on student learning, faculty development, and the campus environment. Survey instruments allow the user to assess faculty and institutional readiness.

Duke Corporate Education (2005). *Leading from the Center: Building Effective Teams*, Dearborn Trade Publishing.

Leading from the Center focuses primarily on teaming: definition, its value, its challenges, and attributes of team leaders. It also includes information on how to work collaboratively and how to manage day-to-day operations.

Smith, K. and P.K. Imbrie (2007). *Teamwork and Project Management* (3rd ed.). New York, NY: McGraw-Hill.

The first chapter of this book, in its third edition, is dedicated to teams, addressing themes related to those in *Leading from the Center. Teamwork* is an excellent aid for building effective teams, and furnishes ample and comprehensive information for implementing your research project from conceptualization tips to evaluation. Instruments are available for every stage of your project along with built-in reflections to improve the process at all stages. The book also incorporates an overview of project management tools from handheld devices to Web-based instruments.

Kaufmann, L. and J. Stocks (eds.) (2004). *Reinvigorating the Undergraduate Experience: Successful Models Supported by NSF's AIRE/RAIRE Program*. Washington, D.C.: Council on Undergraduate Research.

This booklet includes synopses of undergraduate research program case studies from 20 institutions that were funded by the National Science Foundation under the AIRE/RAIRE programs. The case studies address strengthening and broadening participation, curriculum changes, and expansion beyond the participating institution.

Merkel, C.A. and S.M. Baker (2002). *How to Mentor Undergraduate Mentors*. Washington, D.C.: Council on Undergraduate Research.

This work focuses on mentoring undergraduates and describes the attributes of potential candidates, challenges, ethical issues, and practical information on summer and academic year programs, mentoring tips, and research implementation.

Scholtes, P.R. (1995/1988). *The Team Handbook: How to Use Teams to Improve Quality*. Madison, WI: Joiner Associates Inc.

The Team Handbook details numerous aspects of team management from defining team membership roles to establishing a process for continuous quality improvement. This is an excellent resource for every detail of managing teams and its related operations.

Resource Management

Resource management means making adequate resources available to the right people—in this case, group members. Typical key resources for ARGs are lab and office space, supplies, essential books, tutorials, and financial support for travel to conferences. Providing resources is the faculty mentor's job—a job made much easier with administrative support. If they have not already done so, faculty mentors should establish a continuing dialogue with the chairs and deans of their department so that they will be more amenable to investing in undergraduate research efforts. The cost of equipment and financial support for research assistantships can be defrayed by pursuing grants from external sources. Several special grant programs aim to support undergraduate research, many of which are administered through the National Science Foundation and other government funding agencies. The Council on Undergraduate Research (www.cur.org) has a rich array of resources and publications, and many of the articles in the *CUR Quarterly* provide information on programs and funding sources.

Networking

As with any group, the internal dynamics—those among group members—can directly impact the group's productivity and performance. External dynamics—networking outside the group—are also critical. An academic environment offers many opportunities for students to network with other research groups in their academic institution, with other student researchers at conferences, or with visiting researchers.

Internal

The ARG model is built on the cooperative learning paradigm in which students work in groups to maximize the learning of all individuals in the group. As a result, each group member has a vested interest in the success of the others. Group members are also trained to understand the differences inherent in a diverse environment and to appreciate the various personality types and approaches of other members. Structured team activities are designed to reinforce this knowledge. Often, however, faculty mentors must remind team members to appreciate each individual for that person's unique contributions to the group's efforts. Frequently reiterating this principle and encouraging this behavior are particularly important when conflicts arise or during periods of uncertainty, such as when one or more group members leave. Eventually this practice becomes the norm, and all group members accept and value this positive group dynamic.

If positive group dynamics prevail, all group members should exhibit these behaviors:

- initiate discussions and contribute equally in group activities and meetings,
- seek information and opinions from other group members and faculty mentors,
- be willing to compromise and find creative solutions for resolving differences,
- praise and correct other group members as appropriate, and
- accept constructive feedback, whether positive or negative.

Faculty mentors can also raise group members' awareness of how they function in groups by revisiting the "Task/Maintenance Questionnaire," which they filled out in the orientation (see Appendix D, p. 92). This practice encourages students to assess their own behaviors and determine how they can improve their contribution to a positive group dynamic.

External

Faculty mentors can promote external networking by identifying, facilitating, and exploring possible outside connections for the group members. When students have developed their communication and research skills and knowledge and confidence through structured activities, they become remarkably adept at effectively discussing and sharing their work with others. Faculty mentors can aid this growth by supporting students' efforts to attend and give presentations at conferences and workshops, for example.

Day-to-day Operations

Chapter 1 describes the five elements of cooperation that are critical to establishing the ARG environment. Managing an ARG involves establishing a framework to promote student development, which in turn involves five activities, two of which are shown in Figure 5-1:

- research project definition,
- defined deliverables,
- group meetings,
- process improvement, and
- risk management.

These activities repeat as new group members join and are essential for the group's ongoing maintenance. Forms and templates to support these group management activities are in Appendix A.

Research Project Definition

The research project's definition gives students context for realizing the relevance of their assignments. Faculty mentors must take the lead when defining a project,

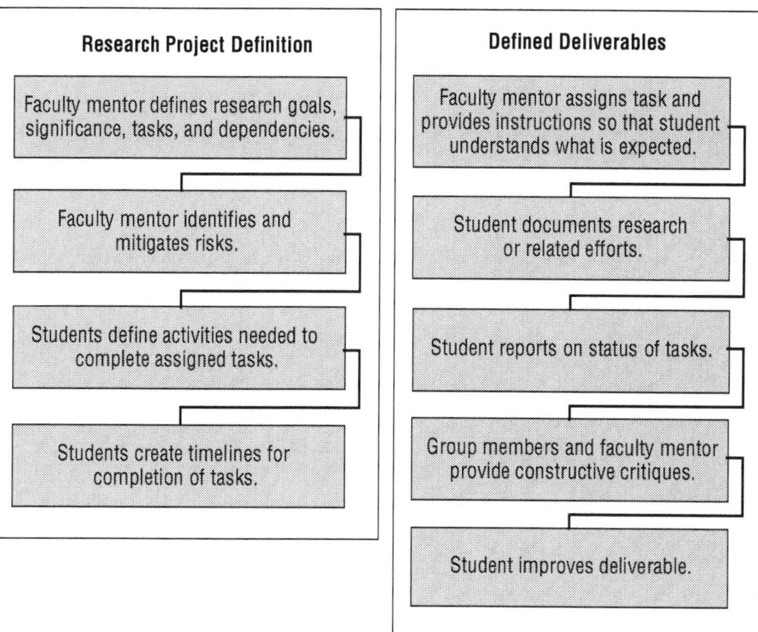

Research Project Definition
Faculty mentor defines research goals, significance, tasks, and dependencies.
Faculty mentor identifies and mitigates risks.
Students define activities needed to complete assigned tasks.
Students create timelines for completion of tasks.
Defined Deliverables
Faculty mentor assigns task and provides instructions so that student understands what is expected.
Student documents research or related efforts.
Student reports on status of tasks.
Group members and faculty mentor provide constructive critiques.
Student improves deliverable.

Figure 5-1: Two of the five activities in managing an ARG. The remaining three are group meetings, process improvement, and risk management.

which means defining both the project goals and objectives and, if the project is part of a larger project, relating those to the larger project. It is important to make the goals and project description readily available by posting them in the research area, on an intranet, or on a website, for example. Faculty mentors can use any number of methods to support a student's understanding of the project. One is to incorporate a unit in the orientation that involves discussing the project with the students. Another is to maintain a repository of background reading material as an annotated bibliography.

At the beginning of each semester, students set personal and research-oriented goals, documenting the activities needed to complete assigned tasks, proposed timelines, and success indicators. For semester-long projects, students must set distinct milestones and discuss them with fellow group members. Timelines are critical to goal setting because they help students define clear goals, evaluate their feasibility, and recognize the balance between research tasks and their coursework. They also help faculty mentors monitor students assigned to multiple tasks.

Project definition benefits *faculty mentors* because they can be certain that students understand the steps needed to complete tasks. Project-definition activities can aid in measuring a student's progress, either formally through status reports or informally during regular meeting times.

> **Learning from Documentation**
>
> Even a simple trip report after attending a conference or visiting another university is an opportunity for students to practice written communication skills such as clarity, coherence, and organization. Moreover, the act of documenting the trip experience increases the potential for learning from it. In writing the report, the student revisits lessons learned and new experiences encountered. By sharing what was learned at a conference, the student transfers those insights to other students in the group.

Project definition benefits *students* because they

- develop the valuable team skills of summarizing and paraphrasing,
- learn to manage their tasks as well as a research project, and
- understand the importance of their work toward completing the project.

Finally, project definition benefits *everyone* by showing task dependencies, which in turn reinforces positive interdependence among group members. This interdependence is one of the five elements of a cooperative group.

An effective practice is to dedicate a meeting (or an orientation component) to discussing the value of defining research goals, setting timelines, and defining deliverables. Faculty mentors can ask students to develop semester-long research plans before the meeting and have students work in pairs or small groups to constructively critique another member's research plan.

Defined Deliverables

Each task has a set of deliverables, which constitute tangible evidence that tasks have been completed and, more important, archive knowledge to be shared. Deliverables help advance the research because fallacies or weaknesses in design or reasoning are more quickly exposed when explanations are written and presented in a cohesive document. Defining deliverables is one strategy for minimizing risks, developing domain expertise, and honing technical and communication skills.

Defined deliverables include products, presentations, reports, and other documentation that group members and faculty mentors can use to determine progress on a project and document discoveries. Examples of defined deliverables are

- abstract or summary of a technical paper or journal article,
- research poster,
- trip report,
- meeting documentation,
- critical review of a journal or conference article,
- technical report or archival paper, and
- creation of a product, such as a software program, research paper, data collection, tool, or proof.

Defined deliverables constitute another approach for establishing individual accountability. Faculty mentors can track research progress as well as hold students accountable for the task assigned to them. For students, deliverables provide an opportunity to contribute tangibly to the research, to integrate domain knowledge (a task that many students find difficult), and to sharpen their technical and writing skills. Students and faculty mentors review deliverables, and the authors of those deliverables must address the identified concerns. Such constructive critiques and revisions are essential for student growth.

In these definition activities, faculty mentors must be sensitive to the student's experience level. For students with less experience, defining deliverables might be an iterative process and faculty mentors must be aware of the time commitment relative to the student's ability. There is a critical balance between the effort to complete a deliverable and the return on that investment.

Group Meetings

The ARG model structures both small- and large-group meetings. Small-group meetings aim to unite students working on similar projects. Large-group meetings aim to work on particular skills and disseminate results from the smaller groups.

Small-group meetings

If an ARG supports more than one distinct project, it is best to break the group into subgroups. Meetings with each subgroup are referred to as small-group meetings and are usually held weekly or biweekly. The objective is to discuss research tasks and advance the research agenda.

At a typical small-group meeting, students discuss the status of assigned tasks and problems they've encountered. Status reporting ensures individual accountability, an essential component of cooperation and keeps other members informed. More important, it gives the group a way to identify problems early enough to prevent lost time. Status reporting can take the form of an informal oral report or submission of reports and formal presentations.

The group members can advance the research agenda by, among other things, discussing technical papers, examining how key ideas from a technical paper relate to the group's research, and brainstorming problem solutions.

The meetings keep students focused and knowledgeable and help the group determine possible changes in research direction. The meetings continually challenge students to discuss their work, which reinforces their understanding of the technical material. This in turn helps the student acquire a depth of understanding in a research area and helps determine if that student can convey knowledge of the material and answer extemporaneous questions. In any one meeting, students might have to teach new concepts, present technical paper summaries, explain milestone research contributions, and describe technical issues relevant to completing tasks. Such discussion develops assimilation skills and helps students

Small Groups

Small-group meetings

- are held frequently,
- allow for discussion of progress made and problems encounter,
- reinforce individual accountability,
- advance the research agenda, and
- are an important arena for the development of student skill.

> **Large Groups**
>
> Large-group meetings
>
> - are held regularly, though not as often as small-group meetings,
> - are an important tool for subgroups to update each other on their progress,
> - facilitate recognition of important group member accomplishments, and
> - constitute an important arena for practicing technical, team, and communications skills.

integrate ideas, possibly by connecting disjointed fields. Group discussion helps students understand the difficulties of research and helps relieve some of the frustrations they might feel.

For faculty mentors, small-group meetings are an effective way to track student progress, promote the refinement of short-term goals, solve problems that students encounter, and help them develop domain expertise. Faculty mentors must structure cooperative behavior during the meeting so that the students can develop their cooperative group skills. For example, mentors can assign the role of gatekeeper to a group member. Another important skill to encourage is constructive criticism—students are reminded to criticize the idea, not the person. Assigning roles can support group functioning, help students assimilate the information being discussed, and help the group foment ideas and resolve conflict. Brainstorming is another useful strategy for getting students to solve the problems they articulate.

Large-group meetings

An ARG with subgroups must have large-group meetings, in which all the ARG members disseminate research results. Such meetings are less frequent than small-group meetings, occurring about two to four times a year. Not only are they a means of integrating the ARG's research results, but they also provide a venue for structured skills development. As Table 5-1 shows, activities can be classified as either research-related (RR) or skills-related (SR), and a large-group meeting can incorporate both kinds.

A large group is an excellent place to practice and critique presentations or technical articles, for example. Before engaging in this activity, the group discusses the criteria for evaluating the presentation or article and its importance. For a presentation, the meeting facilitator gathers the various critiques from the group members and constructively discusses them with the presenter.

Large-group meetings can also be a way to recognize students who have published or presented papers, participated in outreach projects, or received awards. Celebrating individual and team successes is healthy for the group and reinforces positive interdependence.

Process Improvement

Process improvement identifies the strengths and weaknesses in processes and revises processes to address any discovered weaknesses. Process improvement lets faculty mentors assess how well the team is functioning by evaluating the progress of the research, students, and subgroups. Students also benefit because they can self-assess to determine how well they are functioning in the research group. Process improvement also gives them a medium for evaluating their

Table 5-1. Sample activities for large groups and whether they are research- or skill-related (RR or SR) or both.

Activity	RR	SR
At the end of the semester, the group discusses the goals that were set for the current semester, how well the group met them, and what they plan for the next semester. Discuss the meaning and purpose of research, unexpected consequences, and contributions the research afforded.	✓	
Faculty mentors create randomly assigned small groups to brainstorm new ideas for a departmental outreach program. Afterwards, students pick a project on which they want to work and define the task that they will do to contribute to the project. After a particular outreach program, a meeting is devoted to discussing and processing what worked and what needs to be improved.		✓
Faculty mentors and students working on a project, practice brainstorming by identifying research questions and suggesting research directions or solutions to a problem.	✓	✓
Each semester, students give 5- to 8 minute presentations on their current research, including the research goals, significance of work, tasks, and status.	✓	✓
Each student develops a semester-long research plan before the meeting. Students pair with more experienced students and constructively critique another member's research plan.	✓	✓
Students complete a survey designed to gauge each individual's feelings toward working in groups. After students take the survey, the faculty mentor discusses the survey's results. The results are based on how individuals perceive their abilities in task and group maintenance areas. The faculty mentor concludes with a discussion on improving professional skills.		✓

progress and subgroup interactions and for changing their behavior as needed.

Process improvement is the result of a faculty mentor's ongoing efforts to identify students' strengths and weaknesses by continually interacting with them both inside and outside the classroom. Faculty mentors should review their process at least once a semester so that they can understand how well the team is working and make any needed process changes.

Risk Management

Risk identification, assessment, and mitigation are an important part of defining research tasks. One risk typical of ARGs is including undergraduate and graduate students who might be involved in the group for only a short time. Other risks are the possibility that a student will drop a course, lose funding, or decide not to continue in the research program. Risk mitigation in these cases might involve having students work on tasks—particularly those on a critical path—as pairs or trios. Another strategy is to structure meetings in which a member disseminates details about his or her efforts. Yet another approach is to define deliverables that allow information to be transferred among group members and new members, thus preserving continuity and productivity.

Questions for Process Improvement

Faculty mentors could ask students to complete a questionnaire. Based on their responses, they could document the responses received and actions taken or recommendations made. Possible questions include the following:

- Have you achieved your research goals this semester?
- What obstacles have you encountered?
- What has worked well?
- What could be improved?
- Do you have effective working relationships with your group members?
- What member actions do you find helpful?
- What member actions could be improved?
- What can you do to improve your working relationships?

CHAPTER 6: STRUCTURED SKILLS DEVELOPMENT

A major feature of the ARG model is the structured activities that develop the group members' technical, communication, research, and cooperative group skills. The students develop research skills throughout the semester by working with the faculty mentor and through their pairing with more experienced student researchers. Students begin skills development in their area of interest by reading extensively, participating in regular group project discussions, and completing assigned tasks.

Faculty mentors can turn to university services, such as the offices of human resources and development, deans of students, and centers for teaching to schedule a workshop on topics such as leadership or time management, which could be held during a large-group meeting. As the previous chapter describes, large-group meetings are a way to recognize student achievements, to help students develop a broader research knowledge base, and to practice and enhance their technical, team, and communication skills.

Students develop research, technical, professional, and team skills throughout the semester by working with the faculty mentor and experienced student researchers, as well as through assigned tasks. The ARG model relies on structured activities that deliberately address student development in one or more of these areas:

- confidence,
- team skills,
- technical skills and domain expertise,
- written and oral communication skills,
- higher level thinking skills, and
- research skills.

Structured activities might include creating a research poster; critiquing the work of others; becoming an expert in using a particular method, approach, or tool; discussing technical papers; extending previous work; learning from others; managing the bibliographic database; working in tandem; and writing a technical report.

The rest of this chapter contains summaries of each activity. While all activities contribute to many of the aforementioned skills, each summary highlights the primary skill that is developed. All activities build confidence.

Create a Research Poster

Primary Focus: Communication skills

Description: Students create and present a research poster at some venue and answer questions about their research project. Posters provide a way to highlight what individual students are doing, as well as to inform others about the research being done in the group. Many institutions, organizations, and conferences sponsor a research

On Being Well-Prepared for the Rigors of a Fast-Paced, Results-Driven Work Environment

It [an ARG alumna's workplace] is a really tough environment if you're not prepared...You know Affinity group was pretty nurturing, but also demanding. I mean [our mentor] demanded a lot from us. And so I think that that definitely prepared me. Not being afraid to ask questions ... but also just in terms of learning how to communicate; how to write ...
(Former ARG student)

Scientific and Engineering Processes

Scientists attempt to acquire new knowledge through research. The scientific process is based on reasoning about observable, empirical, and measurable evidence. Other professionals, such as engineers, inventors, mathematicians, theoreticians, and computer programmers, have different objectives and follow a different process in their work. Science is concerned with understanding how nature works. Engineering is concerned with the creation of things. Although the exact process a professional uses depends on the area of study, the various approaches have similarities.

Observe

In science and engineering, research begins with observation. The process of science begins with some observation for which there is no scientific explanation. It tries to identify, define, and answer a testable question that will lead to an explanation. An important aspect of science is that the question be testable. That is, data can be collected and analyzed to arrive at an answer. An engineer observes a situation and asks, "What would solve this problem?" or "How can this be made better?"

Conduct Background Research

The next step is to learn about the topic, a process frequently referred to as "background research." For scientists, learning about previous experiments and theories related to the question helps them avoid replicating both the successes and failures of previous efforts. The result of the background research and planning is a hypothesis (a testable question) and an experiment designed to answer the hypothesis. For engineers, the result of background research is the ability to recognize existing products and their strengths and weaknesses. Engineers must clearly articulate engineering goals and identify a plan for developing and evaluating the new product. In mathematics, the result might be a conjecture that must be proved. For computer scientists, the result might be an algorithm and a set of metrics for evaluating the algorithm. Approaches to conducting research include but are not limited to case studies, mathematical modeling, statistical analysis of existing data, participant observation, thought experiments, and direct experiments.

Perform the Work

After establishing the hypothesis or work plan, the logical next step is to do the work—whether that is to conduct experiments, construct a proof, implement a computer program, or build a new

poster session, and students should be encouraged to submit their work. The faculty mentor instructs students that a research poster presentation must clearly and effectively communicate the results of their research to a particular audience in a format that invites interaction and discussion. Poster content and organization will vary, depending on the project type and development stage.

Audience: All research group members. The task can be assigned to an undergraduate or a graduate student, or a group.

Deliverables: (1) A poster that includes an abstract, statement of purpose, results, and conclusions and (2) an oral presentation of the information. Figure 6-1 shows a possible poster layout.

Benefits: For the student, benefits include the opportunity to develop technical, research, collaborative, and written and oral communication skills; to understand the research project's broader impact; and to gain expertise

product. It is important to collect and record the data accurately and without prejudice. Most scientists keep detailed notes of every experiment, measurement, and observation. Such data is essential when they look back at experiments to evaluate their success or when they look at aspects of the problem that they had not considered during the experiments.

Analyze the Data

Once the experiment is complete or the product is built, it is time to analyze the data. The research should answer the hypothesis and lead to a clear explanation of the initial observation. Some questions to ask are the following:

- Did the experiments yield the expected results?
- Were the experiments conducted exactly the same way each time?
- Are the results reproducible?
- Does data have other patterns that need to be explained?
- Were there experimental or observation errors?

For an engineering product, another question might be, "Is the product better than other solutions according to established evaluation criteria?" Analysis frequently requires the use of statistics. It is important to keep an open mind: It is never acceptable to alter results to fit a theory. Some of the greatest breakthroughs in science have been achieved following experiments that yielded unexpected results.

Document the Process and Results

To disseminate the results of research, it is necessary to document the experiment and the result. One way is to prepare and publish a research paper. A good research paper organizes data, explains the research question, and provides enough detail for another investigator to attempt to replicate the experiments.

Based on "Science Research and the Process of Science," http://www.sciserv.org/isef/primer/scientific_method.asp and "Scientific Method," http://en.wikipedia.org/wiki/Scientific_method. Accessed January 2007.

in creating a poster. Students must be able to explain and answer questions that might be posed at a conference or by peers. This helps refine their extemporaneous speaking skills. For the research group, the benefit is integration of research results.

Challenges: (1) Stating information succinctly, (2) understanding the audience's knowledge level, (3) creating appropriate graphical representations, and (4) for the faculty mentor, finding time to proofread the student's work.

Write a Technical Report

Primary Focus: Communication skills and technical expertise

Description: The faculty mentor assigns a student the task of writing a technical report to document advances in research or results of a literature review on a specific topic. See Appendix C, pp. 76-80, for applicable handouts and forms.

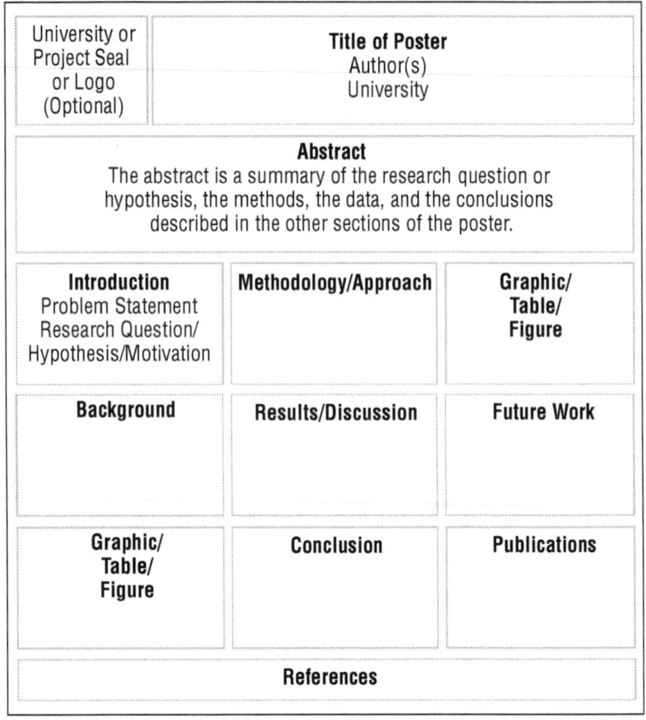

Figure 6-1: Research poster.

Audience: Undergraduate or graduate students.

Deliverables: A technical report.

Benefits: For the student, the benefit is the opportunity to develop research and written and to some extent oral communication skills (because of the need to respond to peer reviews). While writing a technical report, the student will begin to understand the value of publishing research results, how research builds on previous research accomplishments, and the value of library resources. This new knowledge will serve students well, since at some point, they are likely to work on research that requires building on their results. Requiring students to write technical papers at least once a semester forces them to apply skills acquired in other classes, particularly from English composition and technical writing.

The papers are peer-reviewed, which provides the students with useful feedback for improvement. Papers go through numerous reviews and revisions. Each activity requires students to integrate knowledge and skills from multiple tasks and settings to achieve the desired outcome.

For the research group, the benefit is the availability of a research resource and an expert who can teach others how to conduct a literature review.

Challenges: Time required to develop the student's technical writing skills.

Discuss Technical Papers

Primary Focus: Research skills

Description: Students read and critically review papers related to the research project using a form such as the "Journal Paper Summary" and "Literature Review Summary" forms (see Appendix C, pp. 77, 79) to guide their critiques. The appendix also includes "Literature Review Guidelines" and "Tips for Writing a Research Abstract," which are useful handouts. Students come to a group meeting prepared with three questions about the paper. In a student-led discussion, the group looks at the paper and reviews.

Students read a technical paper and prepare questions to give to the student leader before the meeting. The student leader summarizes the paper and facilitates the discussion of it, including discussion of each student's set of questions. The faculty mentors call on members to explain concepts that are unclear to newer members. The student leader prepares an extended abstract and summary of the paper that includes a consolidated review, points of interest for the research group, and new research questions. Faculty mentors review and edit student summaries until they have sufficient quality. Summaries are stored in a repository accessible by the group, where the repository could be a simple text file that can be reached through the group's website.

A variation of this activity might be more suitable for large groups. In the variation, the faculty mentor divides students into groups of three or four, with each group having a mix of graduates and undergraduates. To ensure that all students engage in discussion, the faculty mentor assigns cooperative roles, such as idea integrator and answer summarizer (see Chapter 1 sidebar "Roles to Support a Professional Environment"). The faculty mentor discusses the expectations for these roles before forming the groups.

Again, students read the paper beforehand and come to the meeting prepared to discuss it. The faculty mentor assigns discussion questions to the groups, which come together after a set time to discuss each small group's response.

Audience: All students; this task is well suited to a team that includes either undergraduate or graduate students or both.

Deliverables: An annotated bibliography entry into a repository that includes an extended abstract, a review of the paper that includes points of interest for the research group, and new research questions.

Benefits: For the student, the benefits are the opportunity to practice leadership and oral and written communication skills, and to gain a deeper understanding of concepts and terminology. For the research group, the benefit is exercising higher-level thinking skills in the process of formulating questions.

Challenges: Identifying a technical paper in which the author presents the material at a level that the students can understand.

Critique Work of Others

Primary Focus: Technical and domain expertise

Description: Students critique another student's oral presentation, paper, or experimental design. The presentation critique evaluates content, execution, extemporaneous speaking ability, and professionalism. The paper critique evaluates the paper's contribution to the body of knowledge, soundness of work, support for current research, and how well the paper articulates future research questions.

Before assigning students the task of critiquing a presentation or other artifact, the faculty mentor explains what constructive criticism is and how to provide it. Students review another student's work and submit their evaluations to the faculty mentor. The faculty mentor meets individually with the student presenter to discuss the critiques. The mentor also provides feedback to the reviewers, if necessary, to help them learn constructive criticism. Writing a review makes students more aware of what constitutes a quality presentation, for example. Students learn how to critique their own work and develop critical analysis skills, and the content critiques advance the research.

One way to conduct this activity is by having a student present a paper he or she plans to submit to a conference. Students read and critique the paper before the meeting; evaluate the paper's technical content, originality, organization, clarity, significance; and make an overall recommendation using a provided critique form (see "Paper Critique," "Presentation Critique Form 1," and "Presentation Critique Form 2" in Appendix C, pp. 82-84). The critique form becomes a deliverable for all students. At the meeting, the author presents a brief summary of the work being reviewed, and the group discusses it, focusing on comments and questions.

Audience: All student members.

Deliverables: For a presentation, the deliverables are (1) a review that evaluates a presentation in terms of its content and execution and the student's extemporaneous speaking ability and professionalism and (2) a completed critique form. For a paper, the deliverable is a written report or an oral presentation.

Benefits: For the student, the benefit is practice in providing constructive feedback. For the research group, it is information for improving presentation skills.

Challenges: Appreciating the difference between criticizing the work and criticizing the person; providing meaningful and useful criticism.

Formulate Technical Questions

Primary Focus: Higher-level thinking skills

Description: Various research subgroups within an ARG create a poster on their projects and display the posters around the room. The faculty mentor asks the group

- What is the purpose of good technical questions?
- Why is it important to ask them?
- What are the characteristics of good questions?

The participants break into groups, and each group's task is to come to consensus (the faculty mentor queries the participants to ensure that everyone understands what it means to come to consensus) on three technical questions about the poster. The mentor writes questions on notes attached to the poster. After a set time limit for reviewing the posters (10 to 15 minutes per poster with a maximum of four posters to be reviewed by any one group), the mentor asks the authors to read a posted question to the whole group. The group evaluates the question—is it a good question or can it be refined? This process goes through several iterations. The mentor can decide to evaluate all questions or just selected ones.

After some preset period, the mentor asks participants to return to their questions and rewrite them on the basis of what they've learned and to give the questions to the poster authors. The mentor can assign roles, such as those described in Chapter 1, to help all members participate and reach consensus.

Audience: All research group members, including faculty.

Deliverables: A poster and set of questions.

Benefits: For the student, benefits include the opportunity to practice asking good technical questions, develop higher level thinking skills, and acquire knowledge about other research projects. For the poster author, the benefits are gaining ideas on how to improve the articulation of his or her research and how to advance its direction.

Challenges: (1) Assigning the groups in a way that ensures a good student mix with varying research experience levels, (2) ensuring that the poster discussion is constructive, and (3) structuring the groups so that all members participate and reach consensus.

Define Timelines

Primary Focus: Research and project management

Description: In a meeting with the faculty mentor, the students set personal and research goals for the semester. The faculty mentor assigns tasks for a semester or year, and the students define task activities and a timeline for completing the tasks. At the end of the year, faculty and students reflect on how well the students were able to

Preparing a Technical Presentation

Focusing on these four areas can improve a presentation.

- **Know your audience.** This will help you determine how much background to provide, what terminology to use, what definitions to include, and what background material to present.
- **Understand its purpose.** You can present a talk for many reasons, including raising awareness of a topic, extending knowledge, and presenting research results. Understanding the purpose of your presentation will help you keep it focused.
- **Present a topical overview.** An overview is an effective way to help the audience grasp the material you will be presenting.
- **Cover essential information.** For a technical presentation, cover the hypothesis or thesis, motivation for and significance of the work, background, related work, results, open questions, and future work.

reach their goals and discuss lessons learned.

Audience: All research students.

Deliverables: A set of goals, tasks, activities, and a timeline.

Benefits: For the student, the benefits are learning how to relate the steps in the scientific process to the steps of doing research and practice in setting realistic goals. For the research group, the benefit is the ability to review dependencies.

Challenges: Helping students set realistic semester or year goals.

Give a Technical Presentation

Primary Focus: Communication skills

Description: The student prepares a formal technical presentation based on his or her topic, and the audience is asked to critique the presentation using "Presentation Critique Form 1 and "Presentation Critique Form 2" (see Appendix C, pp. 83, 84). The faculty mentor debriefs the student after the presentation using the critique forms to provide constructive feedback to the presenter.

Audience: All research students.

Deliverables: A formal presentation and completed critique forms.

Benefits: For the student, the benefits are gaining experience in organizing and presenting technical material as well as answering questions; understanding constructive criticism and processing to improve presentation skills. For the research group, the benefits are being more aware of common mistakes in presentations, learning how to provide constructive feedback, and gaining skill in asking questions.

Challenges: For undergraduate students who are presenting a technical paper for the first time, identifying papers that they can understand.

Develop Expertise

Primary Focus: Technical and domain expertise

Description: The faculty mentor assigns a task designed to increase the student's expertise in using a tool or performing a skill that other students in the research group need to get their jobs done. For example, the faculty mentor gives a student the task to learn a new approach, method, or tool. The mentor goes over fundamental concepts, and the student must then pursue knowledge on his or her own by reading and using manuals and online documentation, for example. Once the student has acquired sufficient expertise, he or she can teach learned concepts to the other ARG members. A faculty mentor should be at these teaching sessions to ensure that the students ask probing questions and gain the necessary information from the session.

Audience: Ideal for an undergraduate student

Deliverables: A technical report and a presentation to

members of all ARG subgroups at a monthly meeting.

Benefits: For the student, the benefits are the opportunity to interact and become more familiar with other group members, develop written and oral communication and technical skills, apply inquiry, appreciate the value of documentation, and increase confidence and a desire to learn more about the topic. For the research group, the benefits are the availability of a written resource and an expert who can teach others a technical skill.

Challenge: Matching the task with the student's capability

Support Existing Research Projects

Primary Focus: Research skills

Description: The faculty mentor assigns a student a task that supports the research of others in the group. Because the task is designed to be supportive, the faculty mentor must ensure that the task is well defined and that at least one other person in the group can help the student learn the topic.

Audience: Students beginning a research project.

Deliverables: Depends on the task but may be a design document, a presentation, or document that describes an experimental method and results.

Benefits: For the student, the benefits are the opportunity to develop technical, research, collaborative, critical analysis (in the case of literature review), and written and oral communication skills; to better appreciate documentation's value; to increase confidence; to improve performance in related courses; and to gain practice in goal setting and time management. For the research group, the benefits are acquiring a more experienced research group member who can support increased continuity of the project.

Challenges: Ensuring that the student performing the task gains sufficient background to contribute to the group's body of knowledge.

Learn from Others

Primary Focus: Team skills

Description: Correcting a document manually is time consuming and, if modifications are major, requires another meeting to explain the changes. With the "Learn from Others" activity, a small group reviews a document and, as a student suggests a change, the student explains the reasoning behind the change. Anyone can enter the discussion, which benefits everyone in the group. After a session, the student should be able to make other changes to the document, using the newly gained knowledge and understanding of what faculty mentors expect.

A variation is the use of Whimbey's Paired Problem Solving Method (Whimbey and Lochhead, 1985) that targets teaching skills. This approach involves two roles,

Research Apprentice

To acquire the necessary knowledge to become involved in research, a student may start by working on tasks that support the research. These tasks develop the student's sense of responsibility, timeliness, and resourcefulness, as well as his or her technical, research, and leadership skills.

Tasks could include web page development, literature searches, and participation in an experiment (conduct a survey or collect data). As students become involved in the research project, they are likely to interact with students who are well versed in the subject area.

Ideally, over time the student will be able to contribute more tangibly to the project by extending the research and completing other high-level activities such as co-authoring and presenting papers at conferences.

the problem solver and the coach. The problem solver verbally walks through the problem-solving process so that the coach can understand the process. The coach listens to and coaches the problem solver while seeking to understand the problem-solving process. Working together, the two develop both critical analysis skills and domain expertise. The approach builds on a principle that experienced teachers are familiar with: Teaching deepens the understanding of the topic.

Audience: Beginning students and an advanced student with prior knowledge of the research project

Deliverables: Depends on the task, but may be a revised design document in which the students have applied changes to areas not covered in the review on the basis of what they have learned.

Benefits: For the student, the benefit is the opportunity to develop technical, research, collaborative, critical analysis, and written and oral communication skills. For the research group, it is advancement of research and the development because of the student researchers' increased expertise.

Challenges: Evaluating foundational knowledge and determining when a student is ready to proceed alone.

Work in Pairs

Primary Focus: Team skills and technical expertise

Description: Two students collaborate, review, and critically analyze each other's work. The faculty mentor assigns one student to lead the effort. Deliverables can be assigned to the pair as well as to the individual student.

This activity is key to mitigating risk in ARGs. Ideally, a faculty mentor assigns this activity to two advanced students who have a working knowledge of the research project. If one student cannot continue with the project, continuity is still preserved through the remaining student. This is particularly important for a task on a critical path.

Audience: Advanced research students such as upper-division undergraduate or graduate students.

Deliverables: Depends on the task.

Benefits: For the students, the benefits are the opportunities to develop technical, research, collaborative, critical analysis, and technical writing skills and to gain practice in goal setting and time management. For the research group, the benefit is decreased risk for the group, since if one student leaves another remains who can understand and extend the work.

Challenges: Defining realistic timelines, managing time, and applying collaborative skills apart from meetings with faculty mentors.

Present a Chalk Talk

Primary Focus: Communication skills

Description: The student presents a talk using only a chalkboard or whiteboard—no notes or slides. The audience can ask questions at any time during the presentation. A variation is for the student to prepare an elevator talk, essentially describing his or her research in the time it takes an elevator to go from one floor to another (about 30 to 60 seconds).

Audience: Undergraduate or graduate students.

Deliverables: A presentation that group members can reuse during an impromptu discussion of the research.

Benefits: For the student, the benefits are a refined ability to discuss the assigned research topic succinctly, as well as the opportunity to practice oral presentation skills; to deepen his or her understanding of the research; and to learn which research areas are not well understood and which have potential flaws. For the research group, the benefits are knowledge about research being conducted in the group and practice in seeking understanding and asking questions.

Challenges: Ensuring that the student can present technical material and anticipating areas that the student finds difficult to articulate.

CHAPTER 7: EVALUATING THE RESEARCH EXPERIENCE

The intended audience of this chapter is project directors (PDs), principal investigators (PIs) or researchers and professionals who are interested in the evaluation of the research experience for graduates and undergraduates. The chapter provides a guide that is designed to help the PD conduct simple evaluation and work more effectively with evaluation specialists if and when they come on board. The guide can facilitate the following three roles of the PI/PD in evaluation:

- to evaluate or guide the total evaluation of the program,
- to conduct or guide pre-evaluation or pilot evaluation work that provides immediate knowledge about the program for program improvement, demonstrates the worth of the investment (accountability), and provides information about how activities are working, and
- to select and work with an evaluator to assure that institutional knowledge of the program, its operation, goals, and the intended use of evaluative information is taken into account in the evaluation.

As part of the ARG model, faculty mentors will want to evaluate the effectiveness of their groups, and PDs will want to evaluate the program as a whole. The framework allows flexibility in approaches while at the same time providing a systematic plan for evaluation of an undergraduate or graduate research experience project.

Purposes of Evaluation

Evaluation is the systematic collection of information about program (project) activities, processes, and outcomes for improving the program, and informing decisions about future programs. A good evaluation should: help with the planning, setting up, and carrying out of the program; document the evolution of the program; examine how the program functions within its setting; and assess the short- and long-term results of the program.

In general, evaluation seeks information to

- improve program activities, processes, and outcomes,
- be accountable by rendering judgment about the overall merit or worth of the program, and
- develop an understanding of how elements of the program impact participants and enhance the effectiveness of the program.

Evaluation is retrospective. The reporting of evaluation findings emphasizes the observed performance of a program in relation to what has happened. An evaluation should provide information that leads to statements about what happened in the original site, and what to expect if the original site chooses to improve its plan of action or other sites choose to implement the plan of action (Cronbach et al., 1980).

The overarching concerns that guide an ARG evaluation are as follows:

- What impact does ARG participation have on students' ability to succeed in research, to work effectively in groups, and in the case of undergraduates, to seriously consider graduate school as an option after receiving their undergraduate degree?
- How have activities and the ARG structure increased the number of students successfully engaged in research and influenced students who are not typically involved in undergraduate research?
- What impact does ARG participation have on students' ability to succeed in the workforce after graduation?

Use of Findings

The evaluation literature generally distinguishes two major uses of findings or information from evaluative efforts. Formative evaluation is directed at using findings to improve the program. Summative evaluation is aimed at making judgments about the success or worth of a program. To clarify the uses of evaluative information, consider these concepts in another context: Formative evaluation is when the cook tastes the soup to see if it needs more salt (an eye toward improving the soup); summative evaluation is when the guest tastes it (judging the overall success of the recipe). Scriven (1991) attributes this clarification to Robert Stake.

Just as the different uses of the information are needed to improve a cook's culinary expertise, the different uses of information are needed to assess a program. Both formative and summative evaluations are concerned with program processes and outcomes, but the information they provide leads to very different types of inferences and decisions. The following discussion provides an example of how the information about the ARG has been used for formative and summative purposes.

Formative Evaluation: How Can We Improve?

In the context of a research program, formative evaluation might examine how students are being socialized into the research community. This can encourage mentors to watch for both intended outcomes and unanticipated consequences of student participation. For example, the following questions were used to guide evaluation for the purposes of improving the ARG program:

- How is continuing in or leaving the program a function of students' characteristics, implementation of program activities, and the requirements of student participation?
- What are the essential elements of good student-faculty mentor relationships in an ARG-oriented research experience?

In examining the findings for the on-going evaluation of the ARG, it was discovered that companies and other faculty tended to heavily recruit students who were participating in the ARG. On the basis of this type of information, the project had to address these external pressures. Actions taken included providing students with information on the benefits of continuing to graduate school and developing activities that instilled in them a desire and commitment to completing the research they had started. As the project continued, information from the formative evaluation contributed to an understanding of the essential elements and best practices of an undergraduate research experience that is guided by the cooperative learning paradigm and open to a diverse population of students.

Summative Evaluation: Have We Succeeded?

In the context of undergraduate research programs or projects, information from a summative evaluation could focus on the return on investment and the worth of the program or project. For an ARG assessment, evaluation findings on the impact of participation can be used to address the following questions.

- Did participation in the program increase the number of students who pursued graduate studies? What aspects of the program were instrumental in increasing the likelihood that undergraduate students showed high levels of interest in and application to graduate programs?
- Did participation in the program increase faculty understanding and the implementation strategies for working with students particularly those who are first in their families to pursue graduate degrees?

An Evaluation Framework

The framework for evaluating the ARG uses the continuous improvement cycle of Plan-Do-Check-Act (Deming, 1986). The explicit articulation of the design and development of each phase of the cycle is preceded by a formulation phase that provides the ground work for the conceptualization and implementation of each phase of the cycle.

Table 7-1. Program/Project Description Template.

Evaluation Questions
What do you want to know about your program or project?
Context
What are the needs of the target population(s)?
What are the political, economic, and social realities? Their potential for assets or obstacles?
What are the resources available to support the evaluation?
Goals/Objectives
What is the purpose of the program or project?
What are the expected accomplishments?
Activities
What are the program's or project's core activities?
What are the essential elements and processes of the core activities?
How will activities make possible expected accomplishments (outputs/outcomes)?
Expectations
How will the target population(s) change?
How will other participants and/or institutions change?
Did participation in the program increase faculty understanding and improve implementation strategies for working with students who are first in their families to pursue graduate degrees?

Formulation: Laying the Groundwork

The Program/Project Description Template shown in Table 7-1 is a guide for developing a description of a program. Answering the questions in the template in written form provides information for describing the program to interested parties, designing and conducting the evaluation, and reporting and discussing findings.

The Program/Project Logic Map Template shown in Figure 7-1 is another way to describe the program from inputs to outputs and outcomes showing the connection between activities and expected outputs and outcomes. Some evaluators do not use the output and outcome distinction. It's an individual decision. When the distinction is used, the difference is generally that an output is what is delivered (training hours and knowledge and practice delivered for individual and institutional change) and outcome is what happens as a result (actual changes in knowledge, skill, institutional change). A helpful source for a variety of logic maps is Owen and Rogers (1999) and United Way of America (1996). The United Way document is a good source for developing an input, activities, outputs, outcomes logic model as a basis for identifying indicators and measures and reporting outcomes.

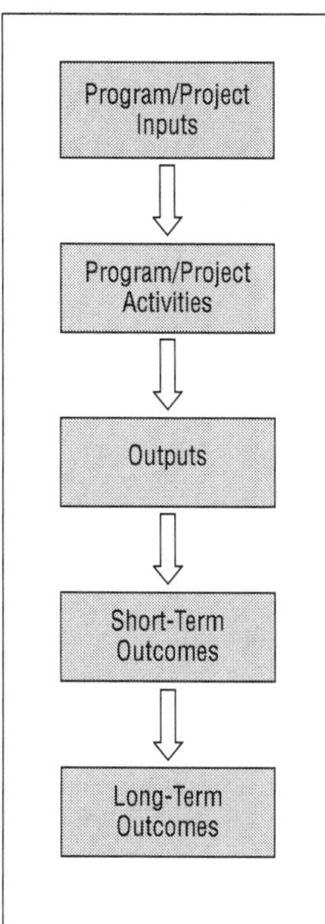

Figure 7-1: Program Logic Map Template.

Most Important Driver: Evaluation Questions

A four-stage approach is suggested for generating and focusing evaluation questions. The intent is to start with what is known to be working and where the "hitches" or problems are. The problems are used to guide the development of specific evaluation questions. Finally, the questions are prioritized with the focus narrowed to make the evaluation feasible.

Stage One: Looking at the Literature

An often-neglected part of designing evaluations is seeing what has gone on before directly or indirectly related to the work. It is helpful in literature review to consider the following steps:

1. Begin with a problem, topic, or focus (it will likely change, but it is good to be clear to begin with since it will guide the search).
2. Collect only those articles that seem sound, focused, and relevant.
3. Summarize the articles and organize them in some classification scheme.
4. Summarize the entire body of literature reviewed being clear about how the literature was selected and con-

structing conclusions about the relevance for and implications for the program and evaluation design (questions, sources of information, variables, methods).

Stage Two: Looking Back at the Program Description

The Program/Project Logic Map and the answers to the questions posed in the Program/Project Description Template support this stage of generating evaluation questions. One should review and reflect on the responses to the questions related to context, goals, activities, or expectations, then determine whether there are any problems or "hitches." Once identified, the problems or "hitches" can be restated in question form.

Stage Three: Matching the Hitches or Problems to Table 7-2 Evaluation Questions

Table 7-2 lists general evaluation questions with each category representing a different program focus. It may be useful to match questions generated in Stage Two to the questions shown in Table 7-2. The table may help in the formulation of more focused questions. The resulting questions are the next refinement of evaluation questions.

Stage Four: Focusing and Prioritizing Evaluation Questions

Not everything can be assessed. Time and cost limit how much can be assessed. But it is necessary to assess what is important for improving or maintaining the culture and productivity of the ARG. Stages Two and Three helped to generate a list of questions. The next stage is to select the most important questions for obtaining the information that will help with the three purposes of evaluation: improving the program, being accountable (demonstrating the worth or merit of the program or project), and understanding (seeing more clearly how elements of the program impact participants and enhance effectiveness). The three steps listed next provide techniques that may assist in the development of assessment questions.

1. Find out where good practice gets trivialized or becomes so routine that one misses the adaptations needed for the context in place. Anyone who has been engaged with professional development teams realizes that there is a tendency for techniques (strategies, tactics, procedures) to become routine and in the process sometimes trivialized, or paid little attention to. As techniques become routine, they are adapted less to a situation. Sometimes this is helpful, i.e., a more efficient or effective procedure is found. Sometimes it is not helpful, i.e., critical parts of a method are left out. In any case, finding these points in a system is one way to focus evaluation questions on things to look at, monitor, or follow up on that

Table 7-2. Sample general evaluation questions (Source: "Utilization-Focused Evaluation," M.Q. Patton, *The New Century*, 1997).

Evaluation Focus	Sample General-Improvement-Oriented Question	Sample Evaluation Question
Program	What are the program's strengths and weaknesses?	What are the structural strengths and limitations of the research experience as implemented in the ARG?
Participants' progress toward outcomes	To what extent are participants progressing toward the desired outcomes?	To what degree have students increased their understanding of research and its practice?To what degree have students increased their ability to participate in or conduct research?
Treatment and participant interaction effects	Which types of participants are making good progress and which types aren't doing so well?	How is leaving or continuing with the program a function of student characteristics and program activities, requirements, and implementation?
Implementation problems	What kinds of implementation problems have emerged and how are they being addressed?	What variables extraneous to the practice of research exert influence on a student's commitment to research and/or on their continuation in computer science?
Unanticipated consequences	What's happening that wasn't expected?	What happens to a student who is now more confident and competent in computer science because of his or her participation in the program?
Social interaction between staff and clients	How are staff and clients interacting?	What are the essential elements of good student-faculty mentor relationships in an ARG-oriented research experience?
Perceptions of the program	What are staff and participant perceptions of the program? What do they like? Dislike? Want to change?	From a student perspective, what are the characteristics of the ARG project when it is working well? When it is not working well?
Perceptions of culture and climate	What are perceptions of the program's culture and climate?	What is the nature of the research culture in ARG as a whole? In the subgroups?
Influence of external environment	How is the program's external environment affecting internal operations?	How does the need for external funding and deliverables affect the way the ARG is adapted and implemented?
Efficiencies	Where can efficiencies be realized?	Can veteran members use informal situations to train and familiarize new members with ARG components and help them socialize with existing members?
New ideas/ adaptations	What new ideas are emerging that can be tried out and tested?	How does the new automated project management tool affect the completion of student projects?
Allocation of resources	How are funds being used compared to initial expectations?	How is faculty time being used compared to initial expectations?
Value added	Is the program providing value-added?	Are students who participate in the program perceived as better prepared to meet the demands of group and independent work situations?
Match with best practices	Do the experiences match what is known about best practices?	How do the ARG activities and structures match with best practices?

will inform on how to improve the program (see Technique 1 in the "Techniques for Further Focusing" sidebar).

2. Locate concerns that come from people using the program (students, professors, others). There are some concerns people have right now. For example, some research group participants may not see themselves (or others) as able to participate in establishing the "core purpose" of the group. In

Techniques for Further Focusing

Technique 1

Look at those parts of the program that have been implemented and are now routine. See if there is a drop off or increase in quality or quantity on key performance indicators. For example, let's say that a research group already has assigned roles and shared goals in working together. Does the group operate according to assigned roles, or has the group changed things? Has that made things better or worse? Does each person know and practice either the assigned role or one that has been substituted by the group as work moved along? This reflection will generate evaluation questions. This is simply one example. What other routines can reviewed?

Technique 2

Ask successful research groups that have designed and implemented a quality research project, what the unique role was of each group member. Then do some backward tracing to find out how things developed to get them to that point. What made the difference? Then ask what seemed to contribute to the successful research? What evidence is there that the training as a research group made the difference? Ask also if anything else going on leads you to believe that continuing in that way will eventually be counter-productive – lead to poorer performance. What questions are generated in this process or refined from earlier ones that are worth pursuing?

Technique 3

Let's say you note in the program description that on "face-to-face promotive interaction" (PI for short) your group does not seem to operate in the suggested way. Members do not always help each other succeed by acknowledging each member's contribution (tacitly or openly), or do not use constructive criticism. Some possible questions for finding out "what is happening" descriptively or "why it is happening" (contingencies) are the following (adapted from Rummler and Brache, 1990, pp. 71-75):

a. Ask the group if everyone knows what face-to-face promotive interaction (PI) is, what they are supposed to do in practicing PI, and how to tell if they are doing it well.
b. Ask the group if there are interferences from other tasks for one's time, or interference from unclear procedures or illogical workflow, or lack of resources that get in the way.
c. Ask the group if the consequences for actions get in the way of doing what you know you should do – a member does not feel following PI pays off in group work, or that there's reward for activities that are counter to PI.
d. Ask the group if feedback on how well people are doing is received as needed, in timely fashion, specific enough, believable, and easy to understand.
e. Ask the group if any shortfalls in quality or quantity of productivity of the group are due to knowledge or skill problems rather than the problems in a to d above.
f. If it is a knowledge or skill problem, is it something that needs special training or could developing a simple checklist or prompting guide make a difference?

addition, some things going on may not be concerns now, but if continued, they may assuredly be concerns later (see Technique 2 in the "Techniques for Further Focusing" sidebar).

3. Find out if any things that are not working are due to lack of necessary knowledge or skills or, on the other hand, if there are problems of execution or application of knowledge or skills people already have. Each node or connection in the program logic map becomes a possibility for thinking of evaluation questions of a

descriptive type (like, "what of importance is happening here?") or of a contingency type ("does this lead to that?"). Analysis of these points may indicate a performance problem there and whether it is a knowledge, skill, or execution problem (see Technique 3 in the "Techniques for Further Focusing" sidebar).

Choosing Methods or Approaches to Collect Information

The method of data collection should match the question. Evidence should be gathered that will support or call into question the claims made about the ARG program or subsets of the research experience within the program. Refer to Penna and Phillips (2005) for the discussion of eight outcome models of evaluation.

This section presents four methods or approaches that are useful for gathering information for program improvement, or for demonstrating to others how the program is working. A variety of methods may be appropriate for a given question. All the approaches described here may make use of document collection, interviews, surveys, focus groups, and observation along with analysis relevant to the questions posed (see "A Cautionary Note" sidebar).

Backward Tracing

This first method uses documents, interviews, and focus groups to look backward and trace how some strong performance got that way. When developing questions, one may find that progress toward outcomes was quite remarkable (based on a question derived from Table 7.1) in some cases for individuals or groups. Or in other cases, it may be found that "good practice" got trivialized. Backward tracing of how things got that way can be done with a combination of document collection (records of what participants were asked to do or planned to do, and did do or reported on doing) and interview (both individual or small group). Kurtz-Milcke et al. (2004) examine cognitive and cultural support in research settings. Dunbar and Fugelsan (2005a; 2005b) study how research is done in the tradition of the sociology of science at the Laboratory for Complex Cognition and Scientific Reasoning.

Real-Time Monitoring

Monitoring progress and events as they occur using a set of indicators of progress developed with input from participants. Monitoring a program or components of a program assumes that there is some set of activities that have been planned and are being implemented. Monitoring is finding out how a program or activity is proceeding along the expected continuum or trajectory toward full and appropriate implementation. An adaptation of

A Cautionary Note

The methods here are intended primarily as descriptive (capturing what is happening or what happened) and classificatory (capturing the structure, or framework, or taxonomy of events or processes). These methods are not intended to formally capture "attribution" of program outcomes to specific implementation variables such as a strong causal methodology might do; however, causal inferences (what does happen under these conditions) and predictions (what might happen in similar circumstances) are often made intuitively by users of evaluative information whenever events are depicted in detail, or in sequence, or in an associative manner. These inferences should presumably be considered hunches or hypotheses to be taken into account for decisions, for actions, or for more formal testing of rival interpretations or conditional statements.

a subset of issues to be considered in monitoring, noted by Owen and Rogers (1999, pp. 239-262) follows:

- Is there a defensible program description? The logic map or other description of the program that was developed with program participants is a starting point. The focus, however, may be on subsets of the total program that are central to your concerns.
- Are there indicators and benchmarks for the program components selected?
- What measures will be used to assess the indicators?
- Is the program or activity under study reaching the target group?
- Is implementation meeting planned benchmarks along the way?
- Are there differences between sites, groups, topical areas, or other comparisons of interest?
- How is implementation now compared with some previous baseline or standards?
- What are the points in the system where "fine tuning" should be considered?

Implementation Characterization

This method calls for descriptive, exploratory, discovery oriented characterization of an implementation within the program. In the ARG context, this may be thought of as an implementation case study. The logic map or program logic may serve as a starting point, but it is unlikely that the case study will cover the entire program. It may be a student, a faculty member, an activity, or a group. Some concern leads to the selection of the case, as suggested in the four-stage approach to questions. As to procedure, there is no simple way to depict case study approaches. See Stake (1967, 1995) for the kinds of data that might be collected in a case study by interview, surveys, observation, or focus group discussions. The general steps for a case study (gleaned from the sources in the "Resources" sidebar) are as follows:

- Construct and refine evaluation questions as suggested in the three-stage process above.
- Decide on the kinds of information to be gathered. Stake (1967, 1995), the focusing down suggestions, and the descriptive evaluation suggestions are all loaded with possible data sources. Data sources must then be selected, such as documents, interviews, focus groups, and quantitative measures based on your "case."
- Design a plan for data collection that is respectful of people's time, privacy, and usefulness of the information.
- Analyze the data with respect to the questions.

- Prepare a report for the intended audience and follow up to ensure productive and sensitive use of the information.

Peer Review

Peer review of the research produced focuses on evaluation of proposals for federal funding of education research projects primarily in the science and engineering context. Understanding the strengths and weaknesses of peer review helps to put the evaluation in perspective. Since the ARG is a research group, having peer review of the quality of the research produced might be one line of evaluation. Since much research today is interdisciplinary or so specialized that it is not easy to find peers knowledgeable about the substantive and methodological areas of a given study, peer review is difficult to arrange. A few key mechanisms follow.

- Find peers who are knowledgeable about the work, or knowledgeable enough to make sense of a review. Historically, a group of peers have different perceptions of quality. Lack of consensus in itself is not a reason to reject peer review. Someone must make sense of the differences in relation to the current context.
- Have agreement in advance as to the purpose of the review and the criteria to be used in the peer evaluation. Presumably it is for the ARG to learn how well they did and where they may improve on the research or the writing of the report. In other words, the purpose is professional development. Being clear about criteria can minimize irrelevant bases for lack of consensus.
- In selecting peers (at least three), minimize conflict of interest, include peers with a variety of perspectives (theoretical or methodological), and include sensitivity to underrepresented groups of students.

Applying Plan-Do-Check-Act

Plan: Creating the plan

Complete or formalize your evaluation plan using the matrix given in Table 7-3. All responses to the previous tasks will provide the information needed to complete a formal evaluation plan.

Do: Conducting the evaluation

This entails following the time-line of activities designed in the planning stage with close attention to management. The unexpected encountered here may tax the management and resource capability as indicated earlier. *The Joint Committee on Standards for Educational Evaluation* (1994) provides a helpful guide to

Resources

Case study may call upon many social science disciplines relevant to education, such as ethnography, psychology, and sociology and there are many approaches. A fairly simple starting approach is also by R.E. Stake (1995). Another source is in Owen and Rogers (1999), especially what they call "clarificative evaluation", Chapter 10, pp. 190-219).

Two key references on peer review are Towne et al. (2004) and the National Academies Committee on Research in Education (2007).

A classic paper by Stake (1967, 1996), "The Countenance of Educational Evaluation," remains an excellent source of information to be gathered.

Table 7-3. Matrix for planning an evaluation.

Evaluation Planning Matrix	
Review of the literature	Select and review relevant, sound, literature for implications for the study.
Questions to be answered by the evaluation	List the evaluation questions that resulted from using the three-stage process for generating, modifying, and focusing evaluation questions.
Uses for the evaluation information	Describe the specific intended uses of the information from the evaluation for one or more of the three evaluation purposes: project or program improvement, accountability or demonstrating worth, and understanding of how the program operates
Audiences for the findings	List the audiences for the evaluation of the program. Who will receive information on the findings?
Outputs and Outcomes Short-term Long-term	Describe the expected intermediate or short-term benefits for the target populations and for those involved in the program.Describe the long-term benefits for the target populations.Describe intended or potential short-term and long-term benefits for populations or institutions not directly involved in the program.
Methods or approaches to your evaluation study	Select an approach for collecting information that will be used in the study. Describe the procedures that will be used to conduct the study using the approach or approaches.
Resources needed: time, personnel, tools, materials, and special budgetary needs.	Prepare a timeline for what is expected to be accomplished for each activity at various points in time. Use the timeline of activities and expected outcomes along the way to estimate needed resources or to modify expectations.

Resources

- **Check.** Frechtling (2002) presents a good summary guide for analying data and interpreting the findings. For qualitative data analysis (though attentive to integrating this with quantitative data), Miles and Huberman (1994) present a broad range of methods.
- **Act.** Wholey et al. (1994) discuss interpretation and reporting to maximize use of information, and Hatry and Kopczynski (1997) provide another practical guide.

use as prompts or reminders of professional and ethical concerns and issues. The standards for utility, feasibility, propriety, and accuracy may all be considered each step of the way in implementation to detect what was missing in planning and to adapt to the realities of context. For example, consider "feasibility" which entails making the evaluation "realistic, prudent, diplomatic, and frugal." This is a reminder to keep disruption to a minimum, to anticipate and take into account "different positions of various interest groups," and to "produce information of sufficient value to justify the resources [expended]."

Check: Analyzing the Data and Interpreting the Findings

The key is close management, accuracy, clarity, completeness, and focus on justification of the claims being made in the presentation of results and recommendations, if any.

Act: Designing for Improvement and Reporting on Worth of the Investment

It is helpful to have a wide range of ways to communicate the results and recommendations of evaluations. For example, one may use oral briefings, short written reports, formal and informal discussions, and technical reports.

REFERENCES

Anderson, A. (1995). Communication from Boeing Commercial Airplane Group. Seattle, WA.

Astin, A.W. (1985). *Achieving Academic Excellence.* San Francisco: Jossey-Bass.

Bandura, A. (1990). "Conclusion: Reflections on Nonability Determinants of Competence," in R. Sternberg and J.J. Kolligian (Eds.). *Competence Considered.* New Haven: Yale University Press, pp. 315-362.

Collins, J.C. and J.I. Porras (1994). *Built to Last: Successful Habits of Visionary Companies.* New York: Harper Collins Publishers, Inc.

Cronbach, L.J. et al. (1980). *Toward Reform of Program Evaluation.* San Francisco: Jossey-Bass.

Deming, W.E. (1986). *Out of the Crisis.* Cambridge, Mass.: Massachusetts Institute of Technology, Center for Advanced Engineering Study.

Deutsch, M. (1949). "An Experimental Study of the Effects of Co-operation and Competition upon Group Process." *Human Relations*, 2, pp. 199-231.

Donath, L., Spray, R., Thompson, N.S., Alford, E.M., Craig, N., and M.A. Matthews (2005). "Characterizing Discourse among Undergraduate Researchers in an Inquiry-based Community of Practice." *Journal of Engineering Education*, 94(4), pp. 403-414.

Dunbar, K. and J. Fugelsang (2005a). "Causal Thinking in Science: How Scientists and Students Interpret the Unexpected." In M.E. Gorman, R.D. Tweney, D. Gooding and A. Kincannon (Eds.), *Scientific and Technical Thinking* (pp. 57-79). Mahwah, NJ: Lawrence Erlbaum Associates, pp. 57-80.

Dunbar, K., and J. Fugelsang (2005b). "Scientific Thinking and Reasoning." In K.J. Holyoak and R. Morrison (Eds.), *Cambridge Handbook of Thinking & Reasoning*, Cambridge Univ. Press, pp. 705-726.

Duke Corporate Education (2005). *Leading from the Center: Building Effective Teams*, Dearborn Trade Publishing.

Frechtling, J. (2002). *The 2002 User-Friendly Handbook for Project Evaluation.* Washington, D.C.: The National Science Foundation.

Gandara, P. (1995). Over the Ivy Walls The Educational Mobility of Low-Income Chicanos. Albany, NY: State University of New York Press.

Gates, A. et al. (1997a). "Building Affinity Groups to Enable and Encourage Student Success in Computing," Proceedings of the WEPAN/ NAMEPA 1997 Joint National Conference. CD ROM

Gates, A., Kubo Della-Piana, C., and A. Bernat (1997b). "Affinity Groups: A Framework for Developing Workforce Skills," Proceedings of the 1997 Frontiers in Education Conference. CD ROM.

Gates, A. et al. (1999a). "A Cooperative Model for Orienting Students to Research Groups," Proceedings of the 1999

Frontiers in Education. CD-ROM.

Gates, A. et al. (1999b). "Expanding Participation in Undergraduate Research Using the Affinity Group Model." *Journal of Engineering Education*, 88(4), pp. 409-414.

Goodwin, T.K., and E. Hoagland (1999). *How to Get Started in Research* (2 ed.). Council on Undergraduate Research.

Hakim, T.M. (2000). *At the Interface of Scholarship and Learning: How to Develop and Administer Institutional Undergraduate Research Programs.* Washington, DC: Council on Undergraduate Research.

Hatry, H.P. and Kopezynski. (1997). *Guide to Program Outcome Measurement: For the U.S. Department of Education.* Washington, D.C.: The Urban Institute.

Johnson, D., and R. Johnson (1989). *Cooperation and Competition: Theory and Research.* Edina, MN: Interaction Book Company.

Johnson, D., Johnson, R., and E. Holubec (1990). *Circles of Learning: Cooperation in the Classroom.* Edina, MN: Interaction Book Company.

Johnson, D., Johnson, R., and E. Holubec (1992a). *Cooperation in the Classroom.* Edina, MN: Interaction Book Company.

Johnson, D., Johnson, R., and E. Johnson Holubec (1992b). *Advanced Cooperative Learning.* Edina, MN: Interaction Book Company.

Johnson, D., Johnson, R., and E. Johnson Holubec (1994). *The Nuts and Bolts of Cooperative Learning.* Edina, MN: Interaction Book Company.

Johnson, D., Johnson, R., and K. Smith (1991). *Active Learning: Cooperation in the College Classroom.* Edina, MN: Interaction Book Company.

Joint Committee on Standards for Educational Evaluation (1994). *The Program Evaluation Standards* (2nd ed.). Thousand Oaks, CA: Sage.

Kaufmann, L. and J. Stocks (eds.) (2004). *Reinvigorating the Undergraduate Research Experience: Successful Models Supported by NSF's AIRE/RAIRE Programs.* Washington, D.C., Council on Undergraduate Research.

Kephart, K., Villa, E., Gates, A.Q., and S. Roach (2008). "The Affinity Research Group Model: Creating and Maintaining Dynamic, Productive, and Inclusive Research Groups." *CUR Quarterly*, 28(4), pp. 13-24.

Kurz-Milcke, E., Nersessian, N.J., & Newstetter, W.C. (2004). "What Has History to Do with Cognition?" *Cognition and Culture*, special issue on Cognitive Anthropology of Science, Chrisophe Heintz, ed. R:663-700.

Lave, J. and E. Wenger (1991). *Situated Learning: Legitimate Peripheral Participation.* Cambridge, UK: Cambridge University Press.

Lave, J. and E. Wenger (1999). "Legitimate Peripheral Participation," in P. Murphy (Ed.), *Learners, Learning and*

Assessment. London: The Open University, pp. 315-362.

McLeod, J. (1987). *Ain't No Making It: Leveled Aspirations in a Low-income Neighborhood*. Boulder, CO: Westview Press.

Merkel, C.A., and S.M. Baker (2002). *How to Mentor Undergraduate Mentors*. Washington, D.C.: Council on Undergraduate Research.

Miles, M.B. and A.M. Huberman (1994). *An Expanded Sourcebook: Qualitative Data Analysis* (2nd ed.). Thousand Oaks, CA: Sage.

National Academies Committee on Research in Education. Retrieved November 29, 2007, from http://www7.nationalacademies.org/core/.

National Academy of Sciences (1987). "Nurturing Science and Engineering Talent: A Discussion Paper." The Government-University-Industry Research Roundtable. Washington, DC.

National Science Foundation (2004a). "Science and Engineering Indicators 2004." Retrieved December 3 2005, from http://www.nsf.gov/statistics.seind04.

National Science Foundation, Division of Science Resources Statistics (2004b). *Women, Minorities, and Persons with Disabilities in Science and Engineering*: 2004 (No. NSF 04-317). Arlington, VA.

Owen, J.M. and P.J. Rogers (1999). *Program Evaluation: Forms and Approaches*. Thousand Oaks, CA: Sage.

Patton, M.Q. (1997). *Utilization-focused Evaluation: The New Century*. Thousand Oaks: Sage Publications.

Penna, R. and W. Phillips (2005). "Eight Outcome Models." *The Evaluation Exchange*. vol. XI, no. 2, pp. 4-5.

Rodriguez, C. (1994). "Keeping Minority Undergraduates in Science and Engineering," *Proceedings of the 19th Annual Conference of the Association for the Study of Higher Education*, Tucson, Arizona.

Rummler, G.A. and A.P. Brache (1990). *Improving Performance: How to Manage the White Space on the Organization Chart*. San Francisco: Jossey-Bass.

Scholtes, P.R., Joiner, B., and B. Streibel (1996). *The Team Handbook* (2 ed.). Madison, WI: Joiner Associates.

Scriven, M. (1991). "Beyond Formative and Summative Evaluation." In McLaughlin, M.W., & Phillips, D.C. (eds.) *Evaluation and Education : At Quarter Century*. Chicago, Ill.: National Society for the Study of Education : Distributed by the University of Chicago Press.

Seymour, E., Hunter, A.-B., Laursen, S.L., and T. DeAntoni (2004). "Establishing the Benefits of Research Experiences for Undergraduates in the Sciences: First Findings from a Three-Year Study." *Science Education*, 88(4), pp. 493-534.

Smith, K. and P.K. Imbrie (2007). *Teamwork and Program Management* (3rd ed.). New York, NY: McGraw Hill.

Stake, R.E. (1967). "The Countenance of Educational Evaluation." Retrieved 8/8/2008 from http://www.tcrecord.org ID Number: 2184. Teachers College Record 68(7), pp. 523-540.

Stake, R.E. (1995). *The Art of the Case Study.* Thousand Oaks, CA: Sage Publications.

Stake, R.E. (1996). "The Countenance of Educational Evaluation." In (Ely, D. and T. Plomp, Eds.) *Classic Writings in Instructional Technology*, vol. 1 pp. 143-160 (2nd ed.). Libraries Unlimited.

Teller, P.J. and A. Gates (2001). "Using the Affinity Research Group Model to Involve Undergraduate Students in Research," *Journal of Engineering Education*, pp. 549-555.

Tinto, V., Goodsell Love, A., and P. Russo (1993). *Leaving College: Rethinking the Causes and Curses of Student Attrition* (2 ed.). Chicago: The University of Chicago Press.

Towne, L., Fletcher, J.M. and L.L. Wise (Eds.) (2004). *Strengthening Peer Review in Federal Agencies that Support Education Research.* Washington, DC: National Research Council.

United Way of America (1996). *Measuring Program Outcomes: A Practical Approach.* Alexandria, VA: United Way.

Whimbey, A. and J. Lochhead (1985). *Problem Solving and Comprehension.* Philadelphia, PA: Franklin Institute Press.

Wholey, J.S., Hatry, H.P., & Newcomer, K.E. (1994). *Handbook of Practical Program Evaluation.* San Francisco: Jossey-Bass.

Wulf, W. (2006). "Testimony to the Commission on the Advancement of Women and Minorities in Science, Engineering, and Technology Development." Retrieved July 16 2006, from http://www.nae.edu/NAE/naehome.nsf/weblinks/NAEW-4NHMH2?OpenDocument.

APPENDIX A

Group Management

Project Summary

Project Name:

Faculty Mentors: Contact information:

Participants: Contact information:

Mission Statement:

Goals:

Objectives:

Division of Tasks:

Timelines and Milestones:

Task Assignment Form

Grant ID: Student Name:

Project Name:

Deadlines: Date started: Date completed:

Tasks:

Dependencies:

List of activities required for completing tasks:

Timelines and Milestones:

Project Status Report

Project Name:

Student Name: | Date:

Task Description: | % Complete

Problems Encountered:

Completed Deliverables: | Stored Locations:

Other Project Successes: | Factors that supported or hindered success:

Research Assistant Agreement

<Semester, Year>

Selection Criteria

A Research Assistant (RA) is an essential member of the Affinity Research Group (ARG). ARG RAs, graduate and undergraduate students, are involved in one or more of the following activities: research, technical support, and outreach efforts for the department, college, and community. RAs are selected on the basis of the following criteria:

1. potential for success in research,
2. academic achievement or capabilities,
3. interpersonal skills, and
4. ability to serve as positive role models to peers and other students.

In order to be eligible for an RA position, a student must be currently enrolled on a full-time basis. Based on university guidelines, full-time is defined as <include guidelines here>.

If an RA's semester GPA drops below the stated minimum, she or he will be placed on probation or terminated at the discretion of the faculty mentors. In the event that an RA fails to achieve the minimum GPA after a semester on probation, she or he will be terminated. RAs should demonstrate commitment to the project as well as acceptable standards of personal conduct and integrity within the department and the community.

Description of Responsibilities and Procedures

The responsibilities of an RA include the following:

1. research activities such as technical paper reading, software development, program simulations, data collection, comparative analysis, experiments, performance evaluation, and/or report writing leading to publication;
2. research-support activities such as literature searches, formatting documents, organizing directories, entering bibliographic data into the research database, and/or web page development;
3. regular attendance at scheduled meetings, as well as departmental seminars;
4. regular discussion and presentation of work in small group, large group, and/or conference settings;
5. teaching of developed skills to other RAs and mentoring junior researchers;
6. facilitation of small and large group meetings, including agenda setting and minute taking; and
7. facilitation of at least one outreach activity per

year.

In terms of the operation of the research group, the following procedures are to be followed.

1. RAs that are funded for 19-20 hours per week are required to complete research-related tasks by assigned deadlines and participate in meetings and activities.
2. RAs are responsible for providing adequate documentation of their work so that other RAs can continue or extend the work.
3. Because projects are funded by several grants, on a periodic basis RAs will report on their progress and will be asked to complete evaluations for purposes of assessment. Faculty mentors anticipate honesty and cooperation in these endeavors.
4. Faculty mentors evaluate RAs on a semester basis. It is the intent of the faculty mentors to provide feedback in order to assist in your continued growth.
5. Outside employment is strongly discouraged due to the significant time commitment required for performance of the RA position in addition to a full-load of coursework. RAs are expected to discuss other commitments with faculty mentors before accepting a position.
6. Eating and drinking in the conference area, main work area, or anywhere near computers or equipment is not permitted. Students are responsible to keep the main work areas and the lunchroom clean.
7. Upon termination of ARG involvement, RAs must return all keys, books, and files to their respective faculty mentor.

Compensation

1. RAs are appointed on a semester basis and receive a stipend or salary commensurate with level of education, experience, and skills. Funding renewal is contingent on RAs' completion and documentation of assigned tasks and end-of-semester interview with faculty mentor.
2. RAs receive instruction concerning the various facets of their position, opportunities for personal development not available to the general student population, and research and technical experience to support their long-term goals.

Code of Conduct

As stated above, an ARG RA must have the ability to serve as a positive role model to peers and other students. It is important that you exhibit professional, ethical, responsible, and courteous behavior since your conduct reflects on faculty mentors as well as other members.

1. The primary use of machines in the laboratory is for research purposes. Machines may serve specific software and, therefore, may be designated for specific projects; students working on those projects have first priority for these machines.
2. ARG members will not port software to machines without the knowledge and cooperation of the system administrators.
3. ARG members will not use software that is not licensed for their use.
4. ARG members will not post any unprofessional materials in their offices.
5. ARG resources are to be used for research and course work only.
6. If for unforeseen circumstances, an RA cannot attend a small or large group meeting, then it is the RA's responsibility to notify his or her faculty mentor.
7. When working in ARG, RAs will be considerate of others by keeping conversation private, not creating excessive noise and distraction, and maintaining clean work and lunchroom areas. For example, using earphones when listening to music shows consideration for others.

Expression of Agreement

By my signature as affixed below, I affirm that I have read and understand the selection criteria, description of responsibilities, compensation, and conditions of employment as stated in this document. I also affirm that all questions I might have with regard to the position of ARG Research Assistant have been answered to my satisfaction and understanding. I am aware that funding is on a semester basis and renewal is contingent on my previous performance. I understand that specific policies and procedures may be modified from time to time as determined by faculty mentors, and I agree that I will respond to any changes as directed by my supervisor(s).

____

Name (print)

____

Name (signature)

____

Date

APPENDIX B

Group Meetings

Table. B-1. Meeting record.

Meeting Record		
Date:	Start Time:	End Time:
Facilitator:		
Recorder:		
Timekeeper:		
Other roles:		
Meeting Agenda :		
1. (min) Review agenda		
2. (min) Review action items		
3. (min)		
4. (min)		
5. (min)		
6. (min) Set date and time for next meeting		
Attendees:		
Action Items:		
Attachments: ❑ Meeting minutes (summary of agenda items) ❑ Carryover agenda items ❑ Other		
Processing of meeting (what worked well and what needs to be improved):		

EXAMPLE MEETING ROLES AND PROCEDURES

Facilitator

When preparing for the meeting, the facilitator is responsible for

- discussing the agenda with the faculty mentor or leader, and
- posting or sending the agenda to attendees.

During the meeting, the facilitator is responsible for

- managing time,
- promoting and encouraging discussion and participation by all,
- keeping the group focused, and
- managing disagreements during the meeting (restating positions, identifying common points and points of contention, and building consensus or tabling discussion until further information can be gathered).

Summarizer

The summarizer is responsible for

- reiterating and clarifying key points (such as task assignments),
- summarizing discussions, and
- asking the speaker to rephrase key points.

Recorder

The recorder is responsible for

- taking attendance,
- reviewing action items,
- noting tardiness, and
- recording meeting minutes and action items.

Group Members

Group members do the following:

- describe their tasks and responsibilities,
- describe and review the milestones that have been reached, and
- set deadlines for next tasks.

Table B-2. Observation Form example.

Observation Form						
ACTIONS	Name 1	Name 2	Name 3	Name 4	Name 5	TOTAL
Contributes ideas						
Encourages participation						
Checks for understanding						
Gives group direction						
Other:						

OBSERVATION FORMS

Observation forms (Johnson et al., 1994) are useful tools for gathering and sharing specific information on how group members work together while completing a task. The form given below has targeted skills listed in the first column. The faculty mentor can observe a single skill or a variety of other skills. Post-its can be used for casual observation.

A summary of the process is given below.

1. Use one observation form for each group. Add names of the students being observed in a group to the first row.
2. Place a tally mark in the appropriate row and column when a student engages in one of the targeted actions. Do not worry about recording everything, but observe as accurately and rapidly as possible.
3. Make notes if something occurs that should be shared with the group, but does not fit into the actions being observed.
4. Write down specific positive contributions by each group member (to ensure that every member will receive positive feedback).
5. Look for patterns of behavior in the group.
6. After the observation period is over, tally the columns and rows.
7. Share the observation form with the group, and ask each member to comment on his or her behavior in the group as reflected by the form. Have the members comment on how the group functioned in general.
8. Discuss how the feedback can help with continuous improvement of the group's functioning.

APPENDIX C

Templates

Thesis Proposal

<Title Page includes the following.>
Title
Author Name and Affiliation
Date
Committee Members

<Proposal body includes the following.>

Abstract

<Include a brief description of the proposed work. The abstract should be 300-400 words.>

1. Introduction

<Introduce the problem and briefly present the motivation for the proposed work. Clearly and succinctly (no more than four lines) state the problem and hypothesis or objective. The hypothesis or objective should succinctly state what you plan to prove or achieve. This section should be no longer than a page.>

2. Contributions

<Describe the significance and expected contributions of the work. Include the broader impacts of the research.>

3. Background

<Present a detailed description of the problem and the conditions under which the problem manifests itself. The scope of the research and the peripheral areas that are excluded from the investigation should be outlined.>

4. Related Work

<Describe and reference related work, i.e., the state-of-the-art in this area, and compare the work with the proposed work. Outline the steps that have been taken to ensure that the proposed research is unique.>

5. Methodology

<Present the proposed plan of work. Briefly describe techniques, approaches, and/or method that will be used to complete the work. It is important to describe a plan for evaluating your work and presenting credible evidence of your results to the research community. Include a timeline with milestones and metrics to measure the success of the research. >

References

<Use APA, IEEE, MLA, or other acceptable citation format used in your area of study. >

Journal Paper Summary

Paper citation: <Citation for the paper being reviewed.>

1. Thesis

<Describe the main point, or thesis, of the paper. Include a brief discussion of what problem is being addressed and what makes the work significant.>

2. Approach

<Describe the approach or methods that the authors use to support the thesis. Approaches include, for example, case study, experimentation, survey, formal proofs, interview, illustration and definition. >

3. Summary

<In your own words, briefly summarize the main points of the paper. Give more detail for those points that you feel are most important and explain why you feel that these points warrant special notice.>

4. Critique

<Describe any deficiencies in the paper and explain the reasoning behind your comments.>

5. Research Questions

<Describe any new research questions that arise from the paper.>

Literature Review Guidelines

A literature review is the process of locating archival publications related to a particular research question(s) and evaluating the results with respect to its relevance and contribution to the research problem.

Sources

- **General references.** The indexes or abstracts in your area that can be used to locate other sources that deal directly with the research question, e.g. the Science Citation Index.
- **Primary sources.** The publications in which individuals that conduct research report the results of their studies. The common primary sources are journals, conference proceedings, and reports.
- **Secondary sources.** The publications in which authors describe the work of others. Common secondary sources are textbooks and surveys.

Steps

- Articulate a precise research problem and questions.
- Formulate pertinent search terms or key words.
- Use secondary sources to get an overview of previous work.
- Use appropriate general references to identify relevant primary sources.
- Record the bibliographical data of pertinent articles using the standard citation style for the research community of interest, e.g., IEEE or APA.
- Review the most recent publications and work backward. Summarize the work, including a description of its relevance and contributions to the research problem.
- Identify relevant references from the publications being reviewed to identify other sources of information.

Literature Review Summary

1. Introduction

<Describe the research problem and research questions. Give the motivation for the research and its significance.>

2. Review

<Summarize the relevant research efforts. Use subheadings to group and discuss related work. Major studies should be described in more detail than less important work. One or two sentences suffice for work that is related, but does not impact the research problem being investigated. >

3. Summary

<Identify the major threads in the reviewed literature and present a composite picture of the results to date. A summary table that categorizes the collected information and its relationship to the research problem with respect to attributes is helpful. >

4. Conclusion

<The researcher may state conclusions he or she feels are justified based on the state of knowledge. What does the literature suggest are appropriate courses of action to solve the problem? What are areas of further research?>

5. References

<Full bibliography for all sources referenced in the review using a citation standard such as IEEE or APA. >

Tips for Writing a Research Abstract

An abstract is a succinct summary of the work being presented. It should guide the reader in determining whether the article or work is of interest. The basic components of an abstract are as follows:

- The research problem and the motivation for the work. Why is the problem important? What practical, scientific, theoretical, or artistic gap does the work address?
- The methods, procedure, technique, or approach that was used in the work being presented. What was done to obtain the results?
- The results, findings, or product that was derived. What new knowledge was learned? Or what was invented? Or what was created?
- The conclusion or implications of the work. What are the broader impacts of the work presented? What new questions have emerged? (optional)

An abstract should be brief. The word count will vary depending on the venue.

An abstract and an introduction have similarities; however, the Table C-1 shows important differences between the two.

Table C-1. Introduction and Abstraction.

	Introduction	Abstract
Main purpose	To introduce the research by presenting its context or background.	To summarize the research, particularly the objective, the results or findings, and conclusions.
Length	Has no hard limit on word count.	Limit on word count (typically).

Proposal Critique

Title:

Author:

Reviewer:

Rate from 1 to 10 (10 being the highest):

Technical Content:
- Research Goal
- Background
- Proposed Work
- Research Plan

Mechanics:
- Clarity
- Organization
- Grammar
- Style

Significance:
- Originality
- Technical Merit
- Broader Impact

Overall recommendations:

Comments:

What is the main contribution of the proposed research?

Guidelines

Basic critique guidelines include the following:

- Keep your review objective.
- Pay attention to the technical organization and content of the paper.
- Comment on the appropriateness of the background, methods, approach, and plan.
- Reject well-written work that will lead to trivial or insignificant results and minor contributions to the subject area.
- Reject papers requiring extensive revisions.

The review is divided into three sections: technical content, mechanics, and significance.

Technical content refers to the understanding of the subject area and the proposed research. Does the author understand current work in the area? Does the author clearly identify an unsolved research question or an area in need of research and development? Is a research or development plan clearly described? Is it feasible? Is a timeline presented? Is the scope of the work clearly bounded? Can the work be completed in accordance with the timeline?

Mechanics refers to the presentation of the proposal. Is the writing clear? Is it free from errors in grammar? Is it written in a professional style? Does the organization make it easy to follow the ideas presented? Is the proposal free from clichés? Is it free from unnecessary jargon?

Significance refers to the impact that the work will have if the research is successful. Is the work original? Does it make a contribution to the field? Is the research technically important or is it trivial? Does it have the potential to impact a large audience either directly or indirectly? Is the research worth conducting?

Paper Critique

Title of Paper:

Author:

Reviewer:

Guidelines:

Keep your review objective.

Pay attention to the technical organization and content of the paper.

Comment on the appropriateness of methods, analyses, results, and conclusions.

Reject well-written papers with trivial or insignificant results and minor contributions to the subject area.

Reject papers requiring extensive revisions.

Rate from 1 to 5 (5 being the highest):

Technical Content:

Originality:

Clarity:

Significance:

Overall recommendation:

Comments:

Comment on the organization and writing style of the paper:

What is the main contribution of this paper?

Presentation Critique Form 1

Name of Speaker:

Date:

On the scale of 1 to 10, where 10 is the highest evaluation, please rate the speaker. In each possible case, note positive and negative remarks that lead to your rating.

Criterion	Rating	Comments
Quality of slides (graphs/figures clear and understandable; text is readable and clear; audio-visual components used effectively)		
Scholarly, informative content		
Interesting, concise, easy to follow and understand		
Centralized focus		
Engaging audience (looks for understanding, maintain eye contact, moves around)		
Appropriateness of detail		
Intriguing (audience interested in finding out more on their own)		
Ability to answer questions		
Overall Evaluation		

Presentation Critique Form 2

Name of Speaker:

Date:

Points	Items	Comments
	Organization (10 pts) * 2 Quality of overheads Parallel structure Consistent fonts Organization and flow	
	Content (10 pts) * 4 Centralized focus Major points covered Appropriateness of detail Understandability Understanding of project Correct use of terminology	
	Extemporaneous speaking (10 pts) * 3 Ability to field questions Content Straightforwardness	
	Professionalism (10 pts) Good pace Minimal extraneous motion Eye contact Language Dress	
	Other (extra credit)	

Overall evaluation:

Recommendations:

Conference/Trip Report

Name: Date:

Event:

Location: Dates of event:

Trip Purpose:

(Please describe the purpose of the trip and, if you gave a presentation, please give the citation of your paper/talk)

1. Summarize the activities in which you participated or sessions that you attended.

2. What was the highlight of the trip?

3. What did you learn from the trip?

4. Would you recommend this conference to other students? Why or why not?

5. List important contacts that you made (name of person, organization, contact information, and remarks).

APPENDIX D

Orientation Support Materials

Sample Agenda for a Four-Hour Orientation

Session 1: Name Tags/Fact Sheet (10 minutes)

Objectives: To introduce students, collect basic information about them, and establish a comfort level and familiarity among all participants.

Activity: Students and faculty mentors complete name tags; students complete fact sheets with basic and contact information. After everyone completes their name tags and fact sheets, faculty mentors ask the students to introduce themselves to other students and to meet three new people.

Session 2: Philosophy and Goals (20 minutes)

Objective: To introduce students to the ARG goals and philosophy.

Activity: The faculty mentor introduces a topic related to the ARG's philosophy, such as the retention of students, and poses a question with a time period for response. One question might be "Why do you think so many freshmen do not make it to graduation?" The mentor instructs students to break into groups of three or four and assigns roles, such as gatekeeper, timekeeper, and recorder, to each member, and discusses the behaviors that characterize each role. (For role descriptions, see Chapter 1 sidebar "Roles to Support a Professional Environment.") After the discussion time is up, one member from each group

Student Fact Sheet

Full Name:

E-mail Address:

Street Address:

City: State: Zip Code:

Home Phone: ( ) Alternate Phone: ( )

- ❑ Undergraduate
- ❑ Master's
- ❑ PhD

Birthday: Faculty Mentor:

Research Area:

Other Areas of Interest:

reports the group's responses while a facilitator records the responses on a flip chart. The faculty mentor then shows students the graphic of the ARG model and discusses the goals and how they positively impact retention and student development.

Session 3: Cooperative team skills (1 hour)

Objectives: To facilitate students' awareness of how they work in groups, to provide a basic understanding of cooperative groups, and to understand and agree upon what constitutes professionalism.

Activity 1: The faculty mentor hands out the "Task/Maintenance Questionnaire" (see Appendix D, p. 92), which students use to score their ability to work in a group. After the students complete the questionnaire, the faculty mentor hands out a scoring sheet (also in Appendix D, p. 93) and engages the students in a discussion of what the scoring means. The mentor then helps the students tie the relevance of cooperative groups to task and maintenance actions. Students keep the questionnaire so that they can track their progress as ARG members.

Activity 2: The faculty mentor reviews the rules of the jigsaw teaching method (as described in "The Jigsaw Teaching Technique" sidebar), gives each student material on the five basic elements of cooperative groups, and divides students into groups of five. Each group member is assigned a number from one to five, corresponding to the five cooperative elements (1: positive interdependence; 2: face-to-face promotive interaction; 3: individual and group accountability; 4: professional skills; and 5: group processing). All students with the same assigned number meet for a set time to learn the material on their particular, cooperative element and each student creates a poster to teach the element to their respective base groups. When the set time is up, the students return to their original group, and each member teaches the others.

Session 4: Research Activities and Skills I (1 hour 15 minutes)

Objectives: To discuss the research goals, process, and infrastructure and to provide students with a framework for understanding these three research facets.

Activity 1: The faculty mentor gives a brief presentation on how to brainstorm, breaks students into groups of three, and tells each group to use brainstorming to discuss the research goals and process. After a set time, the mentor leads a large group discussion of the responses. The students return to their groups of three to discuss the next question—the rewards and challenges of doing research. After the time limit, the faculty member records the responses and again leads the large group in discussion.

Activity 2 (optional): The faculty mentor gives stu-

Name Tags

The organizers select four items that a participant should add to their name tag, as shown in the example below. The name tag serves to identify and introduce participants, and it also supports ice breaker activities. For example, one could ask the participants to introduce themselves to three people who they don't know and to learn why the person has admiration for the one listed on his or her name tag. The facilitator would ask the participants to share what they learned about others.

The example name tag shown below, asks students to list their favorite food, person they admire, accomplishment last year, and life-long goal.

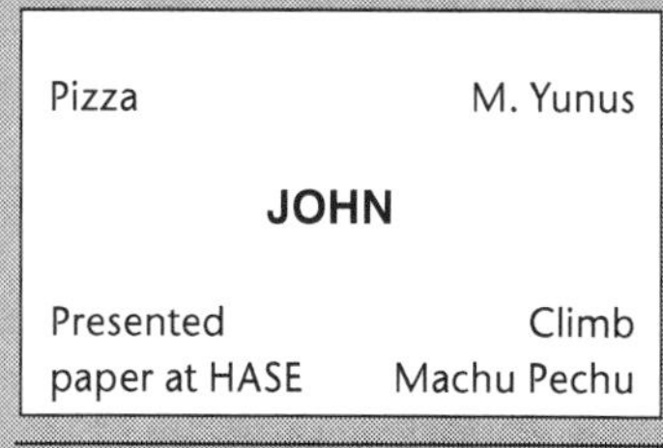

Pizza
M. Yunus
JOHN
Presented paper at HASE
Climb Machu Pechu

Example name tag.

The Jigsaw Teaching Technique

When there is a lot of material for students to review, the jigsaw teaching technique is effective. The steps are as follows:

- Divide the material into thirds.
- Create triads as shown in Figure 1.
- Each member of each triad receives a third of the material. For example, person A in each group gets the same third of the material.
- Provide the instructions: "You each have a third of the material. You will work with a partner from another group and together learn the material well enough to teach it to your group."

Figure 1

- Create preparation pairs as in Figure 2: Person A from group 1 teams with Person A from group 2. If you have an odd number of triads, create a group of three persons.

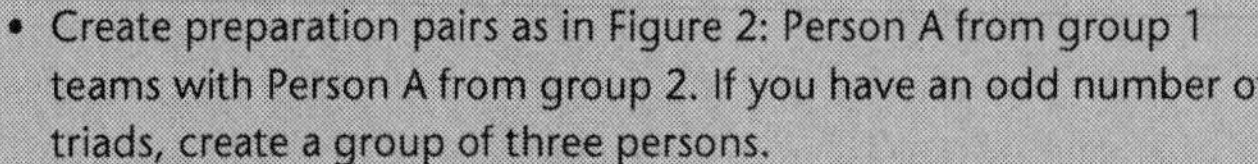

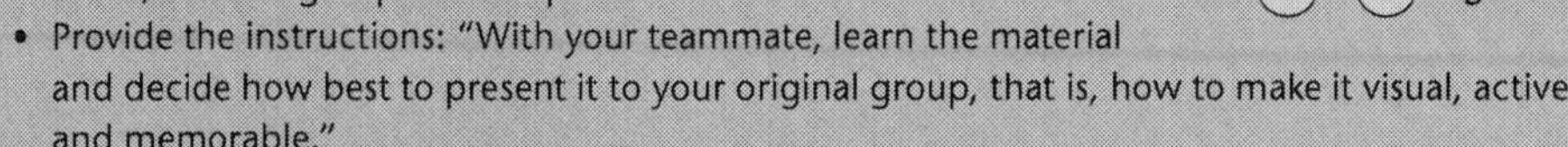

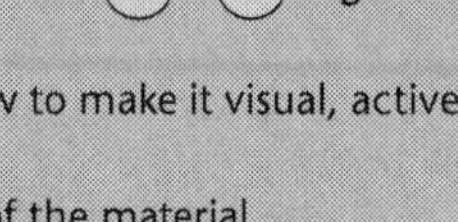

Figure 2

- Provide the instructions: "With your teammate, learn the material and decide how best to present it to your original group, that is, how to make it visual, active, and memorable."
- Allow up to 45 minutes depending on the amount and complexity of the material.
- Return to original triads.
- Teach and learn: triad members rotate in teaching each other for a designated amount of time.
- The whole group is now ready for a discussion of the material as shown in Figure 3.

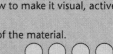

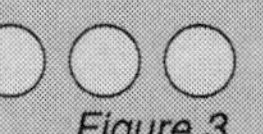

Figure 3

Jigsaw is an effective technique for a group to become intimately involved with the material rather than having a lecture. In this manner, they take ownership and become "experts" of their material.

Adapted from Johnson et al. (1984), *Cooperation in the Classroom*. Edina, MN: Interaction Book Company.

dents copies of the project definition, task record, and status report forms (see Appendix A). In groups of three, the students discuss the value of the forms. This activity is more meaningful if the faculty mentor also discusses the project's mission and goals.

Session 5: Research Activities and Skills II (35 minutes)

Objective: To continue the discussion of research goals and provide students with a framework for understanding the research process.

Activity 1: The new students discuss their responses from the previous sessions with the more senior group members. The faculty mentors facilitate the discussion and add input where appropriate.

Activity 2: Faculty mentors put students in groups of three: each with two old members and one new member. The mentor then introduces the terms *proactive* and *reactive* and asks students several questions: "What do these terms really mean?" "How are they different?" "When is it appropriate to use reactive behavior, and when is it appropriate to use proactive behavior?" After students discuss the answers in their small groups, the mentor leads a discussion involving all the groups.

Session 6: Competing Concerns (35 minutes)

Objective: To discuss and reach consensus about issues that may confront the group and the concerns of group members.

Activity: Faculty mentors place students in groups according to their ARG affiliation or research project. Faculty mentors form a separate group. Using the brainstorming technique, students answer, "As an ARG member, what concerns do you have?" Faculty mentors brainstorm the question, "As a faculty ARG member, what do you expect from a student member of your group?" Each group makes a list and prioritizes answers. To aid this activity, we provide a Nominal Group Technique (NGT) handout (see Appendix D, p. 94). If time permits, a faculty mentor can go over the NGT handout and facilitate the process; otherwise, each student and faculty member is given three stickers and asked to place stickers next to his or her three most important concerns. Faculty mentors and students discuss their respective concerns, relating the highest priority concerns to the ARG model component that addresses them.

Session 7: Evaluation (5 minutes)

Objective: To determine how effective the orientation was in increasing interest in and commitment to the ARG model and in familiarizing students with the ARG concepts, cooperative learning concepts, and research skills.

Activity: The faculty mentor distributes and gives instructions for completing the evaluation of the orientation. Students complete the questionnaire or survey, and return it to the mentor.

Task/Maintenance Questionnaire*

For each question below mark

- 5 if you always behave that way,
- 4 if you frequently behave that way,
- 3 if you occasionally behave that way,
- 2 if you seldom behave that way, and
- 1 if you never behave that way.

Table D-1. Task/Maintenance Questionnaire.

When I am a member of a group:	
1. I offer facts and give my opinions, ideas, feelings, and information in order to help the group discussion.	**5 – 4 – 3 – 2 - 1**
2. I warmly encourage all members of the group to participate. I am open to their ideas. I let them know I value their contribution to the group.	**5 – 4 – 3 – 2 - 1**
3. I ask for facts, information, opinions, ideas, and feelings from the other group members in order to help the group discussion.	**5 – 4 – 3 – 2 - 1**
4. I help communication among group members by using good communication skills. I make sure that each group member understands what the others say.	**5 – 4 – 3 – 2 - 1**
5. I give direction to the group by planning how to go on with the group work and by calling attention to the tasks that need to be done. I assign responsibilities to different group members.	**5 – 4 – 3 – 2 - 1**
6. I tell jokes and suggest interesting ways of doing the work in order to reduce tension in the group and increase the fun we have working together.	**5 – 4 – 3 – 2 - 1**
7. I pull together related ideas or suggestions made by group members and restate and summarize the major points discussed by the group.	**5 – 4 – 3 – 2 - 1**
8. I observe the way the group is working and use my observations to help discuss how the group can work together better.	**5 – 4 – 3 – 2 - 1**
9. I give the group energy. I encourage group members to work hard to achieve our goals.	**5 – 4 – 3 – 2 - 1**
10. I promote the open discussion of conflicts among group members in order to resolve disagreements and increase group cohesiveness. I mediate conflicts among group members when they seem unable to resolve them directly.	**5 – 4 – 3 – 2 - 1**
11. I ask others to summarize what the group has been discussing in order to ensure that they understand group decisions and comprehend the material being discussed by the group.	**5 – 4 – 3 – 2 - 1**
12. I express support, acceptance, and liking for other members of the group and give appropriate praise when another member has taken constructive action in the group.	**5 – 4 – 3 – 2 - 1**

* Johnson et al., 1992 , D., Johnson, R., and E. Johnson Holubec (1992b), *Advanced Cooperative Learning*. Edina, MN: Interaction Book Co.

Table D-2. Task-Actions and Maintenance-Actions Questions.

Score	Task-Actions Questions
	1. Information and opinion giver
	3. Information and opinion seeker
	5. Direction and role definer
	7. Summarizer
	9. Energizer
	11. Comprehension checker
	Total for task actions

Score	Maintenance-Actions Questions
	2. Encourager of participation
	4. Communication facilitator
	6. Tension reliever
	8. Process observer
	10. Interpersonal problem solver
	12. Supporter and praiser
	Total for maintenance actions

Task-Maintenance Scoring Sheet and Patterns

To determine your Task-Maintenance score, add the numeric values for the odd numbered questions and then the numeric values for the even numbered questions. The guide below presents the meaning of the pair (Task, Maintenance).

(6, 6) Only a minimum effort is given to getting the required work done. There is general noninvolvement with other group members. The person with this score may well be saying: "To hell with it all!" Or he or she may be so inactive in the group as to have no influence whatsoever on other group members.

(6, 30) High value is placed on keeping good relationships within the group. Thoughtful attention is given to the needs of other members. The person with the score helps create a comfortable, friendly atmosphere and work tempo. However, he or she may never help the group get any work accomplished.

(30, 6) Getting the job done is emphasized in a way that shows very little concern with group maintenance. Work is seen as important, and relationships among group members are ignored. The person with this score may take an army-drillmaster approach to leadership.

(18, 18) The task and maintenance needs of the group are balanced. The person with this score continually makes compromises between task needs and maintenance needs. Though a great compromiser, this person does not look for or find ways to creatively integrate task and maintenance activities for optimal productivity.

Nominal Group Technique

The Nominal Group Technique (NGT) is an approach that is used to build consensus among team members. In NGT, the group works individually and silently to identify issues, problems, or proposed solutions; they share their most important responses in a round robin fashion; they silently rank the statements of the group after each has been discussed; and last they combine the rankings to generate an ordering of the statements. This process discourages dominance by one or more group members.

The process is as follows.

1. The facilitator explains the process. The group members agree on how the results of NGT will be used, and they agree on who will document the process, results, and any unintended outcomes.
2. The facilitator asks team members to spend five to 10 minutes silently writing down their responses to the topic presented to them.
3. Calling on each member of the team, the facilitator asks the member to contribute his or her most important response. The facilitator records the statement on a flipchart. As with brainstorming, no comments are allowed from the other members.
4. The facilitator eliminates duplicates. Working with the group, the team discusses the statements to ensure that everyone is clear about their meaning. The contributor of a statement should confirm that any revision reflects the intended meaning.
5. The facilitator marks each item on the final list with a letter, starting with the letter "A."
6. The facilitator asks each person to record the corresponding letters on a piece of paper and to rank each

Table D-3. Ranking for consensus example.

Statement	Ranking Person 1	Ranking Person 2	Ranking Person 3	Ranking Person 4	Total
A	4	5	2	2	13
B	5	4	5	3	17
C	3	1	3	4	11
D	1	2	1	5	9
E	2	3	4	1	10

statement according to his or her priority or agreement with the statement. If there are five items to be ranked, then the number "5" indicates the most important and "1" indicates the least important. The reverse ordering helps when individual rankings are combined later in the process. In the following example, "D" is the most important statement and "E" the least:

A. 2
B. 3
C. 4
D. 5
E. 1

7. The facilitator sums the rankings of all team members by letter. In the example given in Table D-3, the ordering of the statements by importance are as follows: B, A, C, E, and D. The results are used as agreed upon by the group in step 1.

Desired Attributes of an Engineer: Boeing Commercial Airplane Group*

- A good understanding of engineering science fundamentals
- A good understanding of design and manufacturing processes
- A multi-disciplinary, systems perspective
- A basic understanding of the context in which engineering is practiced:
  - Economics, including business practices
  - History
  - The environment
  - Customer and societal needs
- A good communicator
  - Written
  - Verbal
  - Graphic
  - Listening
- High ethical standards
- An ability to think both critically and creatively—independently and cooperatively
- An ability and the self-confidence to adapt to rapid change (flexibility)
- Curiosity and a desire to continue learning over a lifetime
- A profound understanding of and commitment to team work

---

*Anderson, A. (1995). Communcation from Boeing Commercial Airplane Group, Seattle, Wash.

An Affective Code of Cooperation*

- Help each other be right, not wrong.
- Look for ways to make new ideas work, not for reasons they won't.
- If in doubt, check it out. Don't make assumptions.
- Help each other win and take pride in each other's victories.
- Speak positively about each other and your organization at every opportunity.
- Maintain a positive mental attitude.
- Act with initiative and courage as if it all depends on you.
- Do everything with enthusiasm.
- Don't lose faith.
- Have fun!

---

*Smith, Karl (2004), *Teamwork and Project Management*, McGraw-Hill.

APPENDIX E

Outreach Materials

Outreach Activity Documentation Template

Activity Overview

<Name the activity, the faculty mentor who is overseeing the activity, and the students involved in creating the activity.>

Goals

<Enumerate goals of activity.>

Summary

<Write a concise summary that describes the activity in general, who the activity is designed for, and what the participants should learn from the activity. If this activity is part of a larger program, briefly describe the program.>

Activity Details and Requirements

<Include relevant information about the activity as listed below.>

Time:

Session length:

Target audience: <Age-group or school grade of students attending session>

Capacity: <Maximum number of participants allowed for one session.>

Facilitators: <Number of facilitators needed and defining characteristics of facilitators if relevant.>

Cost: <Cost of putting the session together (including materials)>

Facilities:

Bldg/Rm#	Room Name	Contact	Purpose

Note: Facilities should be reserved at least 2 weeks in advance.

Equipment and Material:

Item	Contact	Location

Time Schedule and Procedures

The following issues should be discussed in detail so that someone who has never seen the session, but who has an adequate background, can follow the directions and successfully prepare for and facilitate a session.

Preparation

- One-two months before the activity:
  - Who is in charge of the program?
  - How are student participants notified or recruited?
  - Who must be contacted to ensure that your session is a part of the program and session dates/times are adequate?
  - How is the program being advertised?
  - Do posters need to be made?
  - Do facilitators need to be recruited?
- Two weeks before the activity:
  - Should any rooms, labs and/or computers be reserved?
  - What software should be installed?
  - Start meeting with the facilitators to ensure that they understand their role and preparation tasks are evenly distributed.
  - A run-through of the actual session with the overseeing professor and all facilitators present should be scheduled.
- One week before the activity:
  - Are all necessary preparations completed?
  - Should copies of the handouts be made?
  - The run-through should be completed.
- On the day of the activity:
  - How early should facilitators arrive?
  - What last-minute preparations are needed?
  - On students' arrival, what should be done?
  - How is the activity described to the students?
  - What topics should be covered while the students are working in the session and what should the students accomplish in the end?
- Summary
  - Discuss the activity with students and elicit their perspective about the purpose of the activity. Review with them what they just learned or experienced and restate the purpose of the activity.

    Where do students go after the session is over?
- Processing
  - Describe the session's successes.
  - What problems were encountered and how did you work to solve them?
  - What should be improved?
  - What should be done differently next time?

References

- Contact and cited works.

Example Documentation: Be a Robot

The purpose of performing the robot activity is to give students hands-on experience in understanding how a robotics system works and what problems are encountered when programming a robot. Students are divided into teams of four who will work together as a "robot" to build specific structures out of blocks. Each team consist of one "head", one pair of "eyes", and two "hands"(designated left or right). The facilitators for each team should have diagrams of the structures to be built. The blocks and blindfolds should be distributed before the activity begins. One facilitators should show all those playing the "head" the diagrams of the structures. The other facilitators should instruct the "eyes" and "hands" to put on their blindfolds. Once a diagram is shown to the "head", the team should try to build the structure as quickly as possible, according to the role descriptions. Once the teams complete the construction of the first structure, the team should be given another, which is harder to build and so on. Also, the team players should all take turns playing a different role for example the "head" becomes the "eyes" and the eyes become the "hands".

Goals

1. To introduce students to the research and construction of robotic systems.
2. To give students a hands-on experience in understanding how a robotic system works.
3. To show students what problems are encountered when programming a robot.

Example Documentation: Be a Robot (continued)

Activity Details and Requirements

Time: 120 min
Capacity: 16 students (4 groups of 4)
Facilitators: 4
Cost: $50.00

Facilities

Bldg/Rm#	Room Name	Contact	Purpose
CS 300	–	–	To do Be A Robot activity
CS 221	Conference Room		To give the Robot Demonstration

Materials

Item	Contact	Location
Wooden Blocks	–	–
Blindfolds	–	–

Time Schedule and Procedures

Preparation

One week before the activity date, facilitators should reserve a room for approximately two hours. The room should contain two large tables and 16 chairs. Divide blocks into equal sets and put each block set, along with three blindfolds per set, in a plastic bag. Draw four diagrams of the structures to be built out of blocks.

Duration	5 min
Handout	none

On the Day of the Activity

Arrange the tables and chairs in the room into four groups of four, two groups per table.

Duration	5 min
Handout	none

Arrival

Facilitators should guide the students who arriving into the classroom. Wait until there are at least 15 students present (or 15 minutes) to start the activity.

Duration	no set time limit (note: this portion must be completed before the scheduled date of activity.)
Handout	none

Be a Robot Presentation

Begin by explaining the importance of computer science in research and in the construction of robotic systems. Give students a general idea of the positive and negative aspects of robotic systems. Then separate the students into groups of four by counting off. Once students are in groups introduce the roles and rules of the activity (see Appendix D, p. 102). Next, asks if there are any questions about the rules of the activity or the roles each student is enacting (note: if there are not enough students in the group one student can play the role of both "hands" or a facilitator can join the group). Ask all the students playing the part of the "head" to go outside the room and show them a diagram of the structure to be built. Allow students to begin their first attempt at building the structure once everyone has returned to their seat. After all students have finished building the first structure, discuss with them any problems they may have had constructing the object. Next discuss with the students the meaning of ambiguity and communication problems, then define and give an example of an algorithm. Students should repeat the activity, but will rotate the role they played within their groups. In the last ten minutes, wrap the session up by getting feedback from the students on the activity and by answering any questions.

Duration	50 min
Handout	none

Robot Presentation

A facilitator should walk with the students to the room where a presentation on robotic systems is to be given. The students also see a live demonstration of robots.

Duration	20 min
Handout	none

Evaluation

Highlights

- Aerobic name game: In this game, each student says his or her first name while doing an action for every syllable in their name. If the student's name were Sandra the student would say "Sandra" while clapping her hands twice. Then the next student would say his or her name followed by an action and also repeat the name and action of the previous student and so on. This activity was a great icebreaker and enabled students and facilitators to learn each other's names.
- Students showed interest in learning how a robotic system worked and how web pages are created.
- The activities were fun.

Processing

- Facilitators and student's knowledge of the technical aspects of the workshop improved.
- Tasks were made specific and short. That helped maintain the student's attention.

References

The "Be A Robot Activity" was adapted from the activity "Be A Robot" written by Susan H. Rodger and Ellen Walker as a part of the pipeLink program.

Made in the USA
Middletown, DE
15 March 2022

62658193R00064